W9-ARO-544

YOUNG CHILDREN'S THINKING

Studies of some aspects of Piaget's theory

By Millie Almy
with Edward Chittenden and Paula Miller

Foreword by J. Piaget

TEACHERS COLLEGE PRESS
TEACHERS COLLEGE, COLUMBIA UNIVERSITY, NEW YORK

A publication of
The Horace Mann-Lincoln Institute
of School Experimentation
Teachers College, Columbia University

Second Printing, 1967

© 1966 by Teachers College, Columbia University
Library of Congress Catalog Card Number: 66-16091
Manufactured in the United States of America

Foreword

IT WAS with great pleasure that I received the invitation from Miss Millie Almy to write a foreword for her fine book, first because it is an excellent psychopedagogical study, and secondly because it is the first American work to try to apply systematically in the field of education what results I have been able to obtain in developmental psychology.

To begin with I should like to congratulate Miss Almy on her scientific caution. She was perfectly right not to believe me too readily, and to start by carrying out a considerable number of replication experiments, taking off from the many critical or supporting studies which have already been published. Of the research based on my first books (*The Child's Conception of the World, The Language and Thought of the Child,* etc.), I think that the most thorough, which Miss Almy does not seem to have been familiar with, is Laurendeau and Pinard's *La pensée causale chez l'enfant.* [*] These authors have made a trenchant methodological analysis of all the published studies based on these works of mine, and their analysis shows clearly that the studies which support my findings and those which differ from them did not use the same methods of data analysis. Furthermore, the results Laurendeau and Pinard obtained from their own large scale experimentation are of great interest in themselves.

Miss Almy was right also to complement her cross-sectional research with a longitudinal study, which is very interesting and very instructive. It is surprising to me, however, that half of her subjects showed a regression in one or another of the areas she was examining. By contrast, B. Inhelder, with the collaboration of G. Noelting and others, studied thirty children of different ages over four or five years, questioning them every few months on problems of conservation, ordering, etc.,

---

[*] In English translation: Laurendeau, Monique A., Pinard, A., *Causal Thinking in the Child,* International Universities Press, New York, 1962.

and found not a single instance of regression. It is possible that a difference in method is responsible for the difference between these two sets of results. Sometimes a child will react overcautiously to a standardized procedure and give an intermediary response, while a more flexible line of questioning would reveal that these responses did not entirely satisfy him, and that he is capable of going a little further. Above all, the important thing is to see whether the regression, be it apparent or real, is at the level of an intermediate stage, or of a final equilibration, for regression in this second case would obviously mean that in replying correctly in a previous session the subject was not yet really certain of his reasoning, and therefore was in fact at an intermediate stage.

But the chief merit of this work by Miss Almy is to have raised in clear and convincing terms the problems involved in applying these psychological findings to education. I should like to take the occasion which I am offered here to make one or two remarks about these important questions.

A few years ago, the director of the behavioral sciences division of one of the great American foundations, a man prominent in his field but not a psychologist, asked me how I explained the fact that the great learning theories, in the tradition of Hull and Tolman, etc., had had so little influence on the needed changes in education. I replied first that laboratory rats are not the same thing as children in the midst of dynamic development, the more so since they are a degenerated strain which has lost almost all its rodent instincts. But I replied chiefly that the problem of learning is not at all to be confused with that of spontaneous development, even though spontaneous development always comprises learning. It is worthwhile expanding on this point.

For most learning theorists, learning is a primary process: it is independent of development, and mental development is even considered as the sum of successive learning, and not as an autonomous total process. However, such work as was carried out at the Center of Genetic Epistemology* on the learning of logical structures and on the logic of learning seemed to show that for any new logical structure to be acquired, even in a classical learning situation with external rein-

* See "Etudes d'Epistemologie Genetique," Vol. VII to X (*Apprentissage et connaissance*, etc.) Paris, Presses Universitaires de France.

forcement, the subject must be able to call upon other simpler logical or prelogical structures. Otherwise he learns nothing at all from the reinforcement. It appears moreover that all learning—even of a non-essential structure—requires progressive coordination of the subject's own actions, and therefore an internal logic. In other words, in addition to external reinforcements there are indispensable internal reinforcements consisting of satisfactions, feelings of coherence, etc., which follow the surprise or tension due to momentary contradictions.

This is the essential conclusion, as far as education is concerned: learning cannot explain development, but the stage of development can in part explain learning. Development follows its own laws, as all of contemporary biology leads us to believe, and although each stage in the development is accompanied by all sorts of new learning based on experience, this learning is always relative to the developmental period during which it takes place, and to the intellectual structures, whether completely or partially formed, which the subject has at his disposal during this period. In the last analysis, therefore, development accounts for learning much more than the other way around.

But to what factors is development due? Miss Almy emphasizes maturation and experience (both physical and social) and makes much less mention of equilibration as a factor. This is the one, however, that appears to me pedagogically fundamental, and for the following reasons.

First of all, maturation of the central nervous system is certainly a factor until 15 or 16 years of age, but its relative importance decreases with age, because maturation simply opens up possibilities, and never is sufficient in itself to actualize these possibilities. This actualization requires the child's use of the new form, as well as the influence of both the physical and the social environment.

Secondly, when we speak of experience, we must distinguish two different types, which will help us see that a child learns very little indeed when experiments are performed for him, and that he must do them himself rather than sit and watch them done.

On the one hand there is physical experience, which is what everyone thinks of when one speaks of the role of experience in general. This consists of acting upon objects in order to find out something from the objects themselves. For example, in picking things up a child can find out that the weight of various objects is not always proportional to their volume (the beginning of the idea of density).

But there is also logico-mathematical experience. In this case, while the actions are once again carried out on objects, knowledge is derived from the actions which transform the objects, and not from the objects themselves. For example, a child may be surprised to learn that when he counts three groups of two objects he gets the same total as when he counts two groups of three objects. When he learns that the sum is independent of the order of counting he is discovering the properties of the actions of ordering and uniting. He is learning something from these actions themselves, rather than from the objects independent of these actions.

Now, such logico-mathematical experiences require a continual coordination of one's actions so as to keep them coherent and to avoid contradictions. In general, the roots of logic are to be found not at the level of language but at the level of coordinating actions. In this sense of constant self-regulation and self-correction the equilibration factor is fundamental. The equilibrium is to be established among actions and operations (which are simply mental or internalized actions not physically performed); it is not an imposed equilibrium of physical forces as the Gestalt model posits. This constant equilibration, moreover, reveals a remarkable continuity between cognitive functions and organic functions. Contemporary biology has found regulatory mechanisms at all levels, right down to the genome, and intellectual operations can be considered as the highest form of organic self-regulation.

In the realm of education, this equilibration through self-regulation means that school children and students should be allowed a *maximum* of activity of their own, directed by means of materials which permit their activities to be cognitively useful. In the area of logico-mathematical structures, children have real understanding only of that which they invent themselves, and each time that we try to teach them something too quickly, we keep them from reinventing it themselves. Thus, there is no good reason to try to accelerate this development too much; the time which seems to be wasted in personal investigation is really gained in the construction of methods.

Furthermore, the results obtained by B. Inhelder and myself with preadolescents and adolescents have shown that at a certain age children become capable of proceeding experimentally, with systematic variation of factors, so that the whole area of the physical sciences is open to this active kind of education. A number of physicists in the United States are in fact concerned with education of this sort, so we can foresee a good deal of progress in pedagogy, hand in hand with child psychology.

In a word, I am convinced that further progress in this field of psychology will have many repercussions on educational methods, and it is Miss Almy's great merit to have shown this so clearly in her fine work for which I have had the great pleasure of writing this brief foreword.

J. PIAGET

Introduction

PROFESSOR ALMY's *Young Children's Thinking* is the most recent in a series of studies of child development carried on by members of the staff of the Horace Mann-Lincoln Institute of School Experimentation. The first book to come from the Institute was A. T. Jersild's *Child Development and the Curriculum,* followed by his *Children's Interests and What They Mean for Education,* and later by his studies of the self concept, the first of which, *In Search of Self,* dealt with the development of children. Professor Ruth Cunningham did a number of small studies of the social development of children, and finally, in cooperation with teachers in Denver, wrote *Understanding the Group Behavior of Boys and Girls,* which is still widely read. Professor Almy edited and largely rewrote the notes left by Professor Cunningham at the time of her death. This work was published as Almy and Cunningham, *Ways of Studying Children.*

The present study departs from these earlier ones in some respects. First, and most obviously, it deals with the intellectual development of children; the earlier books dealt chiefly with their social and emotional development. Second, it is a longitudinal study, which makes it somewhat unusual in the literature of child development, since longitudinal studies are difficult to develop and maintain. Third, as Professor Almy points out, it depends heavily on the classic work of Jean Piaget, whose studies have received renewed scholarly attention recently. The combination of Piaget's fruitful theories of intellectual development, the kind of rigor implicit in the longitudinal approach, and the freshness of Professor Almy's educational insights, give the study the quality it has.

The members of the Horace Mann-Lincoln Institute staff have appreciated their long contact with Professor Almy during the period of this study. As the work reaches publication, they join with her in a sense of common satisfaction.

ARTHUR W. FOSHAY
Executive Officer
The Horace Mann-Lincoln Institute
of School Experimentation

Acknowledgments

THE PROJECT reported in this volume has received assistance from many sources. It was financially supported by the Horace Mann-Lincoln Institute of School Experimentation. I am particularly grateful to the Institute's director, Professor Arthur W. Foshay, for encouraging the initial exploratory studies and for the many ways he facilitated the completion of the later studies.

Several of my colleagues served as helpful critics throughout the entire project. Professor Arthur T. Jersild, Professor Miriam Goldberg and Professor Elizabeth Hagen were called on especially often. Professor Anne McKillop-Robertson provided many kinds of support, particularly in the planning and exploratory phases of the project. Professor Rosedith Sitgreaves gave invaluable consultation, not only in regard to statistical procedures but also in the interpretation of the data. Professor Myron Rosskopf generously reacted to the report from the viewpoint of a mathematician.

From the first inquiry regarding the feasibility of conducting the major studies in New York City, members of the staff of the Board of Education were most helpful. The Division of Research assisted in locating suitable schools. Principals in the schools gave freely of time and facilities. The teachers, some of them during a three-year period, graciously accepted the interruptions occasioned by the interviewing and aided in the gathering of other information. Thanks are also due the children who made the study possible and in so many ways captivated the interests of the interviewers.

Invaluable assistance in connection with the supplementary studies that are also embodied in this report came from the staffs and children of elementary schools in Englewood, New Jersey, and Manhasset, New York, and of the Agnes Russell School, the Gardens Nursery School and Kindergarten, and the Manhattanville Community Centers in New York City.

In the exploratory phases of the project Carol Buehner, Adele Brodkin, Ascuncion Miteria, Nina Lieberman and Louise Klaber assisted in many ways, and began the observations and interviews that led to the later research. The interviewing for the major studies was done by Jerome F. Brodlie, Sandra Cohen, Beverly Dennis, Miriam Dorn, Margery L. Friars, Felice Gordis, Karen Kessler, Sanvel Klein, Harriet D. Kram, Susan V. Lourenco and Paula Miller.

Although as senior investigator I must bear the responsibility for what is reported here, the project could not have been completed without the collaboration of Edward Chittenden and Paula Miller. Professor Chittenden, now at Mount Holyoke College, shared in planning the major studies, directed important parts of the project and prepared Chapter 6 of this report. Miss Miller made a substantial contribution both in the gathering of the data and in their analysis.

The task of preparing the final report was lightened by Gloria Spencer who did most of the typing.

The reader will have noted the preface written by Professor Piaget. Needless to say, I am extremely grateful for his willingness to read the study and deeply honored by his comments. They have been translated by Eleanor Duckworth, to whom I also wish to express my appreciation. Professor Piaget's preface will, I know, clarify some important issues raised in the study and stimulate further interest in his theories.

M.A.

Contents

CHAPTER 1

The children's thinking project: an introduction

THIS INQUIRY into children's thinking began with observational studies in 1957 and concluded with the completion in 1965 of a longitudinal investigation in which 65 children were studied successively in the kindergarten, first, and second grades.

A major aim at the beginning was to inquire into the effects of classroom experience on the young child's thinking about natural phenomena. As the work progressed, it appeared that an essential step in furtherance of this aim was to make a systematic study of the thought processes of young children of varying age and background, and to explore the educational implications of research regarding cognitive development. This led to a decision to replicate some of the lines of investigation pursued in Piaget's classical studies of children's thinking.

At the time when this decision was made, there was a need for testing Piaget's theories and findings with American children, to provide normative data, and to chart the development of thinking by studying the same children as they advanced in age. There also was a need, from an educational standpoint, to investigate the relationship between the development of cognitive abilities described by Piaget and other mental abilities, as revealed in standardized tests and in school achievement. In addition, there was a need, both from a theoretical and an empirical point of view, to build a bridge between knowledge about children's thinking and what is or might be done in school to cultivate children's thinking.

1

At the present time, some of the needs just named remain as imperative as they were when the project began, while some of the needs have, in the meantime, received considerable attention. Since the initiation of this project interest in the work of Piaget has expanded rapidly. Many research studies, inspired by his theories and findings, have been published in England, Canada, and, more recently, the United States. The Social Science Research Council devoted the entire time of its first conference on intellective development to the work of Piaget. Books by Bruner (1960) and Hunt (1961) delved into the theoretical and educational implications of Piaget's contributions. A volume by Flavell (1963) presented a detailed and comprehensive exposition of Piaget's developmental psychology.

Against the backdrop of the developments in research and theory during the past seven years, the authors' conviction, that exploration of the characteristics of thinking of young children should yield needed information regarding ways of improving their education, has increased. This conviction has dominated the work of the project and given it some of its unique characteristics.

As far as the authors have been able to ascertain, the present inquiry is the first, involving a substantial number of children, to combine Piaget experimentation and a longitudinal approach to the study of children's thinking in an educational setting. The years covered by this study not only represent a significant transitional stage in children's cognitive development, according to Piaget, but also, as is obvious, a very important transitional stage in the child's educational career as he moves from the kindergarten into the primary grades at school.

The present monograph concerns itself primarily with two studies, one cross-sectional, one longitudinal, dealing with the thought processes children display when faced with problems involving the concepts of quantity and number.[1]

The remainder of this chapter discusses the early work of this project

[1] In Piaget's language, these studies deal with children's ability to conserve. Readers who are primarily interested in Piaget theory, as distinguished from its educational implications, may wish to turn directly to Chapters 4 and 5 dealing with the results of the studies of the conservation of number and quantity, and to Chapter 6 dealing with the children's ideas about the floating and sinking of objects.

and the setting out of which these studies emerged. Work presently in progress is also noted.

Preliminary Studies

The impetus for the initial work came from observations in nursery schools, kindergartens, and first grades. These observations indicated that opportunities for stimulating and improving the thinking of the children are often neglected. Failure to nurture intellectual potential was more pervasive in some classrooms than in others, but in almost all of them it appeared that children's interests in the physical world and its natural phenomena received less than adequate support and clarification.

For many years early childhood education has had as an accepted goal the idea of "learning about the physical world." But too often an observer moving from nursery school to kindergarten to first grade is able to detect few differences either in the experiences related to this goal, or in the ways they are presented to the children, or in the ways the children discuss (and presumably think about) them. Yet in occasional instances, one can observe that children make penetrating observations, raise profound questions, and reason in rather brilliant fashion.

We conjectured that the poverty of ideas about the physical world encountered in some classes stemmed more from the paucity of stimulation the children received than from their inadequate or inept thinking. It seemed likely that if the children were given a series of experiences in which they encountered a variety of natural phenomena, and were encouraged both to experiment for themselves and to discuss the results, their thinking might improve. Although initially it seemed that it would be a relatively simple thing to devise an experiment to test this assumption, plans for its execution raised many questions that first had to be resolved.

One major question had to do with the content of the experiences to be offered the experimental groups. Were the experiences and problems typically suggested for elementary school science appropriate? To what extent should they be drawn from the interests or curiosity expressed by the children? Another question was related to the method of appraising the children's thinking and reasoning about natural phenomena.

To arrive at some notion of what might be feasible, a semester was spent observing and interviewing the children in one five-year-old group in a day-care center.

Records of individual children's behavior during play periods yielded some information about the ways the children spontaneously thought about certain natural phenomena, but it was extremely difficult to get adequate samples of such behavior. The interviews, involving the demonstration of certain phenomena to individual children, followed by questions designed to elicit their understanding of what they had seen, were more productive. But the possible relationship between the child's behavior in the play situation and his responses in the interview was often unclear.

Most of the demonstrations and questions used in the interviews in this preliminary study were borrowed from a study by Oakes (1947) which in turn was derived from Piaget's (1929) volume on the child's conception of the world. In addition, two tests, taken from Piaget's later investigations, one dealing with conservation and one with logical classification, were included.

Attempts to classify the children's responses in the interviews led us into further encounter with Piaget's theory. At first we thought surely, as Oakes and other American researchers who had repeated Piaget's early interviews maintained, the child's prior experience was a more important variable in determining the level of the child's thinking than Piaget apparently believed. Further, neither the categories that Piaget used to classify the children's responses, nor the modifications made by Oakes (who noted that he in contrast to Piaget attempted to analyze the nature of the responses themselves rather than to interpret the workings of the child's mind) were satisfactory.

Further study of the interview as a method of gathering data seemed essential.

A more carefully planned but still exploratory study began in the fall of 1958, with most of the data gathered in the spring of 1959. This study involved two groups of five-year-olds, one from a day-care center used in the first study, the other from a nearby cooperative nursery school where the parents were primarily professional. In addition to seeking information regarding the advantages and disadvantages of

THE CHILDREN'S THINKING PROJECT

the demonstration-interview as a method of appraising young children's thinking, the study was designed to inquire into differences in thinking among children differing in school experiences and home background, and in verbal or mental ability. It also offered an opportunity to study individual patterns of thinking as they appeared in the interviews and in the classrooms.

The schedule for the interviews used in this study included demonstrations relating to natural phenomena (air, the floating and sinking of objects, aliveness) and a conservation[2] problem (amount of liquid). The interviews were repeated at the end of a four-month interval, and for most of the children, one year later. In addition students in courses in developmental psychology taught by the senior author used a similar schedule to interview children ranging in age from three through six.

In line with our interest in the relevance of the interviews to the classroom, systematic observational records of behavior in the classroom were kept throughout the first four-month interval. To provide further information, all the children completed the Goodenough Draw-a-Man Test, and the vocabulary test from the Stanford-Binet Intelligence Test. Children in the day-care center were also given the Children's Apperception Test.

The exploratory study inspired a considerable regard for the usefulness of the interview in appraising children's thinking and at the same time a keen awareness of its hazards. On the one hand, we noted how a child might modify his response if we changed the mode of questioning. We also had evidence that the one-to-one relationship with the interviewer meant different things to different children. For some it seemed to be an extension of the classroom, for others a more supporting, or a more challenging situation. On the other hand, the tendency of many children to reveal similar ways of looking at things in different interviews and with different interviewers was reassuring. The interviews seemingly tapped a relatively stable aspect of the children's functioning.

The responses of the day-care-center children provided an interesting contrast to those of the private-school children. As was anticipated, the latter had considerably better verbal abilities. When they

---

[2] The significance of conservation, the ability to grasp mentally those aspects or relationships of a phenomenon that remain invariant or constant over transformations in appearance, is discussed in Chapter 2.

named or described a phenomenon or some aspect of it, their vocabulary was more adequate. But their explanations frequently indicated that they were paying attention to the same things, or were confused in the same ways, as the day-care-center children. Perhaps the most striking difference between the two groups lay in their ability to handle the conservation problem. At the end of kindergarten only one of the day-care-center class of 19 children had conserved as compared with five of the 15 in the private-school group who correctly stated that an amount of liquid remained the same whether it was poured into a shallow dish or remained in a tall glass. At the end of the ensuing year three more children in the latter group achieved conservation, while only one more day-care-center child had grasped the idea that the amount of liquid remained constant regardless of the shape of its container. We began to wonder whether knowledge about their ability to conserve might not provide some important clues for teaching young children, particularly those from disadvantaged homes.

The results of this study were compatible with Piaget's view that the period prior to the age of seven is a period of "intuitive thought," largely based on perception. According to this view the child's thinking in this period consists of a succession of mental images not yet well coordinated to each other. Successively, the child may attend to a particular aspect of an object or an experience, but he is usually unable to deal simultaneously with more than one of these aspects at a time. Consequently, he is hampered in his ability to handle complex relationships or to deal with abstractions.

An attempt to classify the children's explanations in the same way as Piaget had handled explanations of causality in his early publications was not satisfactory. This was not because the children failed to give some explanations closely resembling those described by Piaget but rather because it was too difficult to get agreement among the judges in classifying them. However, when the analysis of explanations was based on a categorization of those aspects of the phenomena that seemed to be in the focus of the children's attention, the ways of thinking revealed were clearly comparable to those described by Piaget in his later works.

The similarities between our children and children described by Piaget were particularly obvious in the explanations of the phenomena of floating and sinking. These could be directly compared with protocols cited by Piaget in *Le développement des quantités chez l'enfant* (Piaget & Inhelder, 1941) and in *The Growth of Logical Thinking* (Inhelder & Piaget, 1958). Typically, the explanations going beyond mere naming of the objects or the water dealt with the properties of the objects or the water. Usually these properties were handled singly, often with no apparent concern for the contradiction involved in attributing the same property to an object that sank, as had previously been attributed to one that floated. Similar difficulties in coping with several variables at once, and in dealing with contradictions, were also apparent in the explanations of other phenomena.

On the whole, the ways of thinking about natural phenomena revealed by the children, and their apparent interest in the attributes and actions of objects, accompanied by some concern for, but not much insight into, causes and relationships, fitted rather well Piaget's description of what he has called the preoperational stage of mental development. On the other hand, some of the results of the study raised questions regarding certain aspects of Piaget's work and its implications for education.

A persistent question in this study had to do with the ways the child's thinking in the interviews resembles or differs from his thinking elsewhere. In *The Child's Conception of the World,* Piaget (1929) devoted considerable discussion to the safeguards that the adult must use in order to avoid suggesting certain answers to the child and encouraging him to perseverate. The more recent *Growth of Logical Thinking* (Inhelder & Piaget, 1958) implies that the child's own demonstration or experimentation provides a better index to the nature of his thinking than do his verbal responses to questions.

A number of years ago, Isaacs (1930) in commenting on Piaget's method of questioning said, "Piaget is digging deeper than he realizes. . . . The child has not yet the organized body of knowledge to resist being pushed back into the realm of phantasy and egocentricity below rational thought. He has not yet built the common-sense scientific world into himself deeply enough to rest upon it when apparently prompted toward his phantasies by an influential adult" (p. 94). The exploratory study tended to support Isaacs' view on this. It suggested that the child's responses in the interview may be importantly influenced by his beliefs about the adult's expectations for him. Some children apparently saw the interview as a situation where the adult was testing their knowledge. But others viewed it as an invitation for fantasy and free association.

Little, if any, research was available to indicate whether a child who, in an interview, gives imaginative and bizarre responses is likely to differ in his play and in the classroom from the child who gives more matter-of-fact responses. Isaacs, in refutation of Piaget's early ideas regarding the limitations in young children's understanding, cited many instances in which they were able to reason in quite logical fashion. Unfortunately, these children cited by Isaacs were not interviewed as well as observed, so no conclusions could be drawn as to the comparability of the interview and the classroom.

In the exploratory study, the children's responses in the interviews were compared with some of their responses in the classroom. Considerable similarity in the levels of performance were found. However, the problems confronting the children in the classroom often bore little resemblance to those they encountered in the interviews. In part, this reflects the fact that the demonstrations included in the interview had not been selected to be representative of the classroom experiences. But it also raised a question as to whether the kinds of limitations in thinking revealed by the children's responses in the interviews were much of a hindrance in the kindergarten that was centered around play.

In this connection, it should be noted that Piaget's ideas regarding young children's thinking appear to have had little if any influence on classroom teachers. Indeed, many teachers with whom these ideas were discussed were reluctant to examine them, and inclined to resist them after they had done so. All of them could cite examples of confusion in the thinking of the children with whom they worked, but they also quoted instances of sound reasoning and good generalization. Their experience seemed to indicate that, whatever the nature of the limitations in the young child's thinking, they tended to be more sharply revealed and more hampering in the interview situation than in the classroom.

We had no classroom data for the children after they left the kindergarten. Judging from their responses in the interviews, however, they tended to become more similar in their thinking than they were in kindergarten, that is, certain explanations became more popular, and there were fewer superficial explanations. The qualitative shifts were not great but they raised several questions so far as Piaget's theory was concerned.

One such question had to do with the nature of the transition from "intuitive," perceptually dominated thought to more logical and more systematic thinking.

According to Piaget's theory the ability to "conserve" number and quantity is basic to such transition. But his studies did not provide satisfactory normative data regarding the age at which such transition might be expected. Nor did they suggest to what extent progress in relating conservation to different kinds of tasks is likely to be made by a particular child since he apparently used different groups of children to study different tasks.

A further question had to do with the effect of experience on the speed of transition. Piaget, in collaboration with Inhelder (1958), had suggested that children in intellectually stimulating environments might advance from one stage of intellectual development to another somewhat more rapidly than would be the case for other children. The evidently better conservation abilities found in our private-school group as compared with the day-care-center group seemed to conform to this possibility. But more evidence was needed.

Studies of Young Children's Conservation Abilities

The ability to conserve is revealed when the child grasps the mathematical idea that number is not changed when a set of objects is partitioned into subgroups, and the physical idea that mass or substance does not change when the shape or appearance of an object is transformed. The attainment of such ability, according to Piaget, marks the transition from predominantly intuitive, subjectively oriented thinking to thought that is more socialized and more like that of the adult. A child who has this ability is more amenable, than one who lacks it, to instruction in the concepts regarded as basic in various areas of knowledge.

Although a major focus in the children's thinking project as it was initially conceived had been to test the effects of instruction on the young child's thinking about natural phenomena, the need to find out how children of different experiential backgrounds thought before receiving special instruction became paramount, and has dominated the subsequent research reported here.

The studies reported in Chapters 4, 5, and 6 were designed to explore the educational significance of children's ability to conserve.

The first investigation set forth in these chapters is the cross-sectional study involving two groups of kindergarten, first- and second-grade children drawn from two schools in different socioeconomic areas of New York City. Each child was given three conservation tasks: two demanding recognition that the number of a set of blocks is not altered when it is rearranged in space; the other the awareness that an amount of liquid does not change when the shape of its container is altered. The child's prediction about and explanations for the floating and sinking of certain objects were also recorded. Other individual measures included the Stencil Design test and the Ammons Picture Vocabulary test. School records provided additional measures of intellectual functioning and academic readiness and achievement.

In the longitudinal study, the kindergarten children from the cross-sectional study were reinterviewed at six-month intervals until they reached the end of the first semester of second grade.

Related Work

During the period when first the cross-sectional and later the longitudinal studies were in progress a number of other activities also went on.

Chief among these has been an exploration of the literature related to Piaget's theories. The task has been at once stimulating, rewarding and frustrating. As Flavell (1962) noted at the first Conference on Intellective Development, a psychologist who studies Piaget never again sees children in the same way. On the whole, we have found that the theory set forth by Piaget serves as a lens that magnifies and thereby clarifies the ambiguities of the child's developing thought processes. At times, however, the view has been as through a glass— darkly.

One who reads Piaget is grateful for and has no difficulty understanding the protocols describing the behavior of the children in his experiments. But Piaget's translation of that behavior into symbolic logic and his lengthy digressions from his theory into other theories, often outdated for the contemporary reader, represent formidable hazards for those who would comprehend him. Since the inception of this study the reader's task has fortunately been facilitated by several comprehensive reviews of Piaget's theory and by an increasing number of studies replicating many of the experiments.

Our own study of the literature has led in two directions. Some individuals associated with the project have become interested in clarifying issues related to specific aspects of the theory. The junior author's (Chittenden, 1964) study dealing with relationships between the ability to conserve and to seriate is an example.

Other work in progress concerns itself with both theory and pedagogical implications. One doctoral study deals with the effects of training on children's ability to grasp a class-inclusion relationship at five, six or seven years of age.[3] Another study involves the abilities underlying the use of a vertical-horizontal coordinate system, and Piaget's concept of "logical multiplication." [4] A third is concerned with children's understanding of concepts of order and sequence.[5]

Much of the work that is a direct outgrowth of the present project has been pragmatic in nature. It raises the question: to what extent can Piaget's ideas assist teachers in planning for and evaluating educational experiences provided for young children?

The senior author has presented her understanding of these to a continuing seminar of kindergarten teachers and supervisors,[6] where some of the members have become sufficiently interested to read some of Piaget's investigations and to try out some of his ways of testing children's comprehension. She has also drawn on Piaget's theory in a continuing consultative relationship with a group of teachers involved in a preschool enrichment program,[7] and in an association with a group of scientists engaged in writing curriculum material for the elementary school.[8]

[3] Paula Miller

[4] Jerome Brodlie

[5] John Swayze

[6] New York Kindergarten Seminar, sponsored by The Bureau of Child Development and Parent Education of the State Education Department.

[7] Institute for Developmental Studies, Department of Psychiatry, New York Medical College.

[8] Minnemast Science Writing Project, summer, 1963; Science Curriculum Improvement Study, University of California, Berkeley, California.

She and some of her students have made and analyzed observational records of children's behavior in classrooms from nursery school through second grade, seeking evidence on their ways of thinking.

Two hunches have emerged regarding the applicability of Piaget theory to early childhood education. One is that the theory provides a convenient framework for deciding on the sequence in which concepts in mathematics or science can be presented. The other is that an overconcern with such sequence may lead to neglect of the important factors of the child's own activity and his interaction with his peers in the transition from intuitive to logical thinking. It is considerably easier to organize instruction around what are presumed to be the cognitive capabilities of an average or typical four-, five-, or six-year-old than it is to match that instruction to the conceptual repertoire of a specified child.

Interviewing young children, observing them in their classrooms, and listening to their teachers have convinced us that teachers can learn to move behind the verbal facade that so often obscures young children's thinking. In further research, and through collaboration with teachers, we hope to investigate what the teacher needs to know and do if he is to accomplish this.

In this monograph our aims are more limited. We deal with one aspect of a child's thinking—his ability to conserve number and quantity as revealed in three tasks, how that ability relates itself to other intellectual abilities and to school readiness and achievement, and how it changes and develops over time.

CHAPTER 2

The development of logical thought in early childhood

THE CHILD's ability to comprehend the principle of conservation (sameness, invariation) as it applies to matter and quantity is, for Piaget, a landmark in the development of logical thinking. Prior to this achievement, the child's thought tends to be dominated by his perceptions. He reasons from one particular instance to another particular instance, and is often unaware when his conclusions contradict one another. Beyond the attainment of conservation, thought becomes more conceptual. The child is less likely to be taken in by the appearance of things. He can deal with more complex relationships, not only taking into account the immediate situation but mentally making comparisons and exploring the similarities and the differences in previous experiences.

All of these differences can be summed up in the statement that the older child has at his command "a coherent and integrated cognitive *system* with which he organizes and manipulates the world around him" (Flavell, 1963, p. 165). The information from his experiences is mentally registered in such fashion that he can readily think his way through them, moving forward or backward at will. He has no difficulty in cancelling out the effects of change in order to focus on the elements of an experience that have remained unchanged.

The younger child, who has not yet firmly established such a system and cannot so readily reverse the direction of his thought is more prone to errors in judgment. The classic example of such error is an "experiment" [1] in which Piaget confronts a child with two balls containing equivalent amounts of plasticene. The child readily agrees that the amounts are the "same," but when one of the balls is elongated into a long thin "sausage," the child, caught up in the perceptual disparity, believes that there is more plasticene in the sausage, or perhaps in the ball. He can not mentally cancel the effects of the transformation in appearance and recapture the original equivalence of the two balls. In Piaget's terms he has not yet achieved *reversibility* in his thought.

The presence or absence of systematic mental manipulation, once an observer has become aware of the possibility of its existence, can be inferred in a variety of the child's behaviors. A kindergarten child, for example, building a "skyscraper" from blocks, puts his toy cars in a "garage" at the bottom, but neglects to construct any means of exit for them. When he wants to get the cars out he has built the structure so high that he can not reach inside it. He tries to solve the problem by standing on a chair, placed against the block wall of his building. An older child, operating more systematically, would hold in mind the original relationship between his own height and the location of the cars and recognize the inadequacy of his idea.

Observant teachers, working with first- and second-grade children, can furnish many examples of the older child's emerging cognitive system. It manifests itself in his lessened dependence on the teacher in the accomplishment of a given cognitive task. The younger child given an assignment that involves, for example, marking an x on the one box in each set of four that contains the "largest" object may become intrigued with x's, and decide to fill all the boxes, or he may become preoccupied with some aspect of the objects other than their size. The older child can not only hold a single guiding idea firmly in mind, but he can make additional judgments appropriately, as, for example, putting a circle around the boxes that contain the largest objects that are made from metal.

Piaget's experiments with children of varying ages reveal some

---

[1] Piaget uses the term "experiment" to refer to the situation in which an interviewer uses the clinical method of interrogation to probe the child's thinking about various kinds of problems. The term is used in this sense throughout this report.

of the elements in the increasing ability to work systematically. The experiments, whether they deal with quantity and number, space and geometry, or with the logic of classification, all reflect the extent to which the child is able to "conserve," and the facility he has in mentally retracing his own cognitive steps. They are so designed as to permit the observer (provided he is sufficiently well grounded in Piaget's theory) to describe the child's cognitive activity in terms of the logical "operations" involved.

The term "operation" has a dual significance. In its mathematical and logical sense it refers to the transformations implied in such symbols as $+$, $-$, $\times$, $\div$, $>$, $<$. In its psychological sense it refers to the mental activity involved in carrying out such transformations. When Piaget speaks of "concrete operations" he indicates that the child is able to perform mentally actions that he has previously carried on in actuality.

However simple an experiment may seem, Piaget can always relate a child's performance in it backward in time to some prior achievement, and forward to an anticipated but not yet realized accomplishment. At the same time he assumes that the level of functioning reached in a particular experiment should also hold for other tasks involving similar logical complexity. Each of the multitude of experiments has its own unique position in the elaborate fabric of Piaget's theory of intelligence. Accordingly, the significance of a particular experiment, or of conceptual tasks derived from his experiments as are those in the present study, can best be understood in the context of his theory.

Piaget's Views of Development and Learning

Piaget, in contrast to most of his contemporaries in psychology, apparently begins his inquiries, not with the learner (whether that be child or adult, monkey or rat) but with knowledge, the substance to be learned. He has, moreover, a pervasive concern with the structure, or logical organization, of knowledge.

The structure of knowledge

Since the term "structure" is used in different senses at different times by both Piaget and by educators and psychologists interested in his theory, a comment on certain distinctions in meaning is in order. Inhelder (Tanner & Inhelder, 1953), in *Discussions on Child Development,* has noted that Piaget is by vocation a zoologist, by avocation an epistemologist, and by method a logician. As a zoologist, Piaget's interest in structure may be presumed to have to do quite directly with the arrangement of organs, tissues, and cells in the body. As an epistemologist and philosopher his interest in structure is more figurative, and has to do with the arrangement of the ideas that go to make up particular bodies of knowledge, such as those of mathematics or physics. Obviously various arrangements are possible, but in regard to any particular body of knowledge, or "discipline," one can expect to find some consensus among its scholars as to the ideas or concepts that are most elementary, and the relationships of these ideas to others more complex in nature. Recent efforts to revise curricula, particularly in the elementary school, represent attempts to help children to understand such basic concepts and the ways they are related, that is, to grasp the structure of the various "disciplines," or areas of subject matter.

Piaget, apparently not convinced that scholars and philosophers can arrive at an adequate picture of the structure of knowledge without reference to the ways human beings come to know, contends that the most basic ideas are those the child is first able to grasp. Knowledge arises and becomes organized as the child interacts with his environment.

Piaget further maintains that the central idea in the structure of knowledge is the *operation.* He explains:

> Knowledge is not a copy of reality. To know an object, to know an event, is not simply to look at it and make a mental copy, or image, of it. To know an object is to act on it. To know is to modify, to transform the object, and to understand the process of this transformation, and as a consequence to understand the way the object is constructed. An operation is thus the essence of knowledge; it is an interiorised action which modifies the object of knowledge. For instance, an operation would consist of joining objects in a class, to construct a classification. Or an operation would consist of ordering, or putting things in a series. Or an operation would consist of counting, or of measuring. In other words, it is a set of actions modifying the object, and enabling the knower to get at the structures of the transformation (Piaget, 1964, p. 8).

Operations, further, are reversible, and always linked to one another. What has been added can be subtracted, what has been joined can be separated. A logical class is part of a total structure of classification; a given number is part of the sequence of numbers.

Piaget's studies of intelligence are designed to reveal the order in which the human being becomes able to perform different kinds of operations or, put another way, to apprehend structures of varying complexity.

Piaget's experiments deal with the observed behavior of the children, and not directly with what may be going on within the brain, but he implies that as behavior increases in complexity, so too do the information-processing structures of the brain and nervous system.

Churchill describes in simple terms the possibilities for such development during the sensorimotor period of development (birth to about eighteen months).

> From birth the little human organism is a responsive system. . . . He has to come to know two worlds, his own inner world and the outer world, and this response is possible because every response he makes is registered in the mental structure which is being built into the system from the beginning. Every new experience, every sensori-motor reaction makes links with comparable experience already registered. Every sensation mediated by the eye is caught and registered on inner structure, so also every movement sensation, every sound attended to, every touch. In this way cell assemblies of knowledge are being built into the mental life of the child . . . information about the shape and size of things, the relation between one event and another, and so on (Churchill, 1958a, p. 36).

In this period, "knowledge" could be said to consist of the repertoire of actions the child uses in response to the objects he encounters. As the child begins to recollect these actions (Piaget speaks of "interiorized images") and as language develops, he enters into a new state: Piaget calls it a stage of *preoperational representation*. It is called "preoperational" because the thought processes representing actions are not yet reversible. Consequently the child's knowledge is not yet systematized. The child may count objects or he may be struck by similarities in the properties of objects, but not until he discovers that his own actions in arranging and disarranging them can be ordered and related, does he really engage in logical-mathematical experience. As Piaget describes it, such experience is "an experience of the actions of the subject, and not an experience of objects themselves. It is an experience which is necessary before there can be operations. Once the operations have been attained, this experience is no longer needed and the coordinations of actions can take place by themselves in the form of deduction and construction for abstract structures" (1964, p. 13).

True operations do not appear until in the third stage when they are labeled *concrete* in contrast to the *formal operations* of the fourth and final stage. The term concrete indicates the extent to which the child's thinking, however logical and systematic it may be, is still bound to direct experience. Though he may no longer need to manipulate actual objects in order to understand their relationships, his thoughts about them are limited to direct experiences he has had. In instances where he has had no direct knowledge he reasons by analogy to something he has experienced.

Truly abstract thinking involving the ability to deal with the possible without reference to the actual is, according to Piaget, a later development. Not until he enters a final stage of *formal operations*, at the beginning of adolescence, can the young person construct theories and make logical deductions as to their consequences without the necessity for empirical evidence. Presumably not until this stage can the complexity of the structure of human knowledge begin to be fully grasped.

Stages in the development of intelligence

Piaget's description of the stages of development can be misleading unless one bears in mind his basic preoccupation with knowledge. To view his stages of intellectual development as descriptive only of the development of the children is to miss his concern with rational activity at the highest levels. For example, he begins *The Child's Conception of Number* (1952a) with a discussion of the contribution of the principles of conservation to the empirical sciences of physics and chemistry. Only after that does he move to consideration of conservation as "the necessary condition for all rational activity" (p. 3).

Whereas, for example, the items in the Binet intelligence test, at least at the early levels, are dependent on practical, common-sense information, Piaget's experiments are designed to lay bare the child's progress toward an understanding of the abstract structures underlying human knowledge. Working with children of various ages with somewhat similar backgrounds, Piaget has identified the sequence in which such understanding seems to evolve.

For the psychologist and educator, the crucial problem, as Kessen (1962) has suggested, is to secure an adequate picture of the transitions that occur in the sequence, and eventually to specify the factors involved in them. If, for example, the typical second grader in a middle class school solves a given conservation task in a way that is totally different from that of his first-grade contemporary, what has propelled him to his new view? Why does an equally typical second grader in a school in a lower class neighborhood continue to function preoperationally throughout second grade and often well into the third?

Piaget is not unconcerned with these kinds of problems and has offered a description of the factors that he believes are involved (Piaget, 1964). On the whole, however, his work reveals a greater preoccupation with unraveling the sequence in which different yet somewhat related concepts are grouped. For example, the volume dealing with the concept of number is paralleled by one dealing with quantity (Piaget & Inhelder, 1942), and by yet another concerned with classes, relations, and number (Inhelder & Piaget, 1964).

In nearly all of Piaget's work, each experiment is followed by protocols illustrative of the various stages and substages. The fact that these are always identified by the ages of the children and that Piaget and his colleague, Inhelder, frequently delineate stages of major development of intellect in terms of ages tends to give the reader the impression that "age" and "stage" are regarded as synonymous. More accurately, age seems to be simply a point of reference, not nearly so important as the implications that Piaget derives from the way the child copes with particular tasks set him. A child who is truly operational in dealing with a quantity of liquid may be expected to handle a problem involving the logical classification of objects rather differently from a child whose thinking is still preoperational. However, it is not clear from Piaget's writing to what extent he has posed similar problems to the same child or group of children. The children whose thinking is described as "operational" in one experiment are, it appears, not necessarily the same children as those who are labeled "operational" in experiments dealing with different but related concepts.

Consequently the question of whether the levels of thought are actually as pervasive and as clearly demarcated for individual children as they are set forth in Piaget's theoretical formulation must remain open until the results obtained when each child completes an array of different experiments are known.

Factors involved in transitions

Piaget's (1964) description of the transitions from one stage to another, and indeed from one substage to the next, includes four main factors. The first is *maturation*, the increasing differentiation of the nervous system. The second is *experience* with the physical world. The third, *social transmission*, involves encounters with other human beings, and more specifically, education. The fourth, *equilibration*, or self-regulation, is for Piaget the fundamental factor.

Something of what Piaget has in mind when he refers to the factor of equilibration or self-regulation can be inferred from his views on the relationship between development and learning. For Piaget, learning is a process provoked by external situations (a psychological experiment, a teacher, some exigency of the environment) and limited in scope. The child learns "a single structure," or solves a single problem. Such learning is subordinate to development. Development is not, for Piaget, the sum or the culmination of a series of specific items. Rather, "development is the essential process and each element of learning occurs as a function of total development, rather than being an element which explains development" (Piaget, 1964, p. 8).

Accordingly, a child in a given conservation experiment may learn to give a conserving response, indicating that a given amount of clay remains "the same" regardless of whether it is formed into a ball, elongated, or broken into pieces, but fail to reach a similar conclusion when the same problem is posed at a different time, or under different circumstances. Conceivably he may return from the conservation experiment and choose to break up his lunchtime cracker in order to have "more" to eat. The child's "learning," or in Piaget's terms, his verbal *accommodation* to the demands of the task, has had no lasting effect, nor has there been any generalization to other tasks. The child has been through an experience, but he has not *assimilated* it and it has in no way affected his ways of organizing his experience.

Such "learning" may be contrasted with the situation in the conservation experiment where the child responds to the interviewer's question with steadfast assurance that a given amount of substance remains "the same" regardless of the transformation it undergoes. Such assurance may even imply that the adult must be slightly addled to raise doubts about the matter. At this point it becomes clear that the child has a new way of handling incoming information, a new "structure," in Piaget's terms. Previously the child paid attention only to the way the clay was arranged in space. If it was spread over a large area it was in some way different. Now, presumably primarily as an outcome of his own manipulation of those and similar materials in many other situations, he has constructed a new dimension from which to view them—a stable amount or quantity. Many of the children's responses indicate this when they say, "It *looks* different, but it's the same amount." The *accommodation* to the external environment involved in the physical experience of handling objects in a variety of ways has now been balanced by mental *assimilation* of the information. One might say (Wohlwill, 1964) that the child has a new "set" toward a number of intellectual tasks.

The crucial fact for Piaget seems to be that this "set" or attitude must come from within. What is learned at any given point is, at least in part, determined by what has gone on before, not merely by what the child has experienced, but more by the elements to which he has paid attention. "Every instruction from without presupposes a construction from within" (Flavell, 1963, p. 406).

To the psychologist, seeking the rules governing transition from one stage of intellectual development of thought to another, and to the educator, concerned with propelling the child from a given level of thought to some higher level, Piaget's insistence on equilibration or self-regulation is at once provocative and frustrating.

Some of the frustration arises from the difficulty involved in comprehending all that Piaget means by equilibration. Self-regulation, a term that Piaget (1964) has recently used as an alternative expression does not quite capture the complexity involved in his usual statements of his theory. Essentially, it seems, equilibrium represents the point at which the processes of accommodation (fitting one's behavior to the demands of the outer world) and assimilation (changing the patterns of organization of the inner or mental world to encompass the information obtained through accommodation) are in balance. But it is not clear how much discrepancy between the demands from without and the structure from within is necessary to disturb equilibrium, nor what impels the child toward restoring it. To assess the maturational and experiential factors that contribute in some, as yet not specified but nevertheless important, fashion to what Piaget terms equilibration or self-regulation seems exceedingly difficult.

On the other hand, Piaget's experiments in themselves provide the needed diagnostic tools for appraising where a child is in his thinking, and where he perhaps might go next, even if they reveal only grossly how he got to where he is. In any event, the ferment of Piaget's views among both psychologists and educators seems unlikely to abate until they have undergone far-reaching examination. The present study attempts examination of one aspect of those views, namely the significance of the conservation of number and quantity in intellectual development during early childhood.

The Child's Conception of Number

The Child's Conception of Number, originally published in French in 1941, but not translated into English until 1952, provided the experiments from which the conservation tasks used in the present studies were derived. The volume illustrates admirably both the nature of Piaget's theories and his methods of working with children. Although it can not be characterized as easy to read, teachers, among others, have found it somewhat less difficult than some of Piaget's other writing.

Flavell (1963) states that Piaget's number research has a very broad base. In turn, the number research provides support for the work in other areas. *The Child's Conception of Number* (Piaget, 1952a) is a companion piece to *Le développement des quantités chez l'enfant* (Piaget & Inhelder, 1941). These two volumes bear a direct relationship to two later volumes, *The Early Growth of Logic in the Child* (Inhelder & Piaget, 1964) and *The Growth of Logical Thinking from Childhood to Adolescence* (Inhelder & Piaget, 1958). Piaget, in his foreword to the *Conception of Number,* says, "Our hypothesis is that the construction of number goes hand-in-hand with the development of logic, and that a pre-numerical period corresponds to the pre-logical level" (p. viii). In *Quantités,* Piaget explores the intellectual processes involved as the child reveals the ability to conserve substance, weight, and displaced volume. He notes how the operations involved in dealing with these properties parallel the operations involved in understanding logical classification (combining on the basis of "sameness"), and in understanding seriation (ordering on the basis of difference). These operations are, in turn, basic to the development of the concept of number, since the latter involves recognition of the fact that the objects in a collection can be regarded as both equivalent in some way, and orderable in some way. *Quantités* deals with discontinuous quantity; *The Child's Conception of Number* gives initial consideration to some of the same ideas and experiments and then moves forward to test their applicability in dealing with sets of objects, or discontinuous quantities.

Cardinal and ordinal aspects of one-one correspondence are then considered, and, in the final sections, various relationships between number and logical classification are investigated.

Crucial to the child's mathematical understanding and indeed to all his rational activity, in the view of Piaget, is his grasp of the principle of conservation, an awareness of whatever remains the same when something changes.

"Whether it be a matter of continuous or discontinuous quantities, of quantitative relations perceived in the sensible universe, or of sets and numbers conceived by thought, whether it be a matter of the child's earliest contacts with number or of the most refined axiomatizations of any intuitive system, in each and every case the conservation of something is postulated as a necessary condition for any mathematical understanding" (Piaget, 1952a, pp. 2–3).

Conservation of continuous quantity

The experiment with which Piaget begins his inquiry into conservation is the now classic test where the child is given two cylindrical containers of equal dimensions containing the same quantity of liquid. The contents of one container are then poured into two smaller containers of equal dimensions and the child is asked whether the quantity of liquid that has been poured out is still equal to that remaining in the other container. Many variations can be played on this experiment by subdividing the liquid in various ways. Or, Piaget indicates, as a check on his answers, the child can be asked to pour into a glass of a different shape a quantity of liquid the same as that in a given glass.

Piaget's results indicate three stages of understanding. In the first, there is no evidence of conservation. The child's responses indicate that the quantity of liquid increases or decreases according to the size or the number of the containers. Sometimes he notes the level of the liquid, and says that the quantity has diminished. Sometimes the number of smaller glasses seems to lead him to believe that the quantity has increased. Again, he may pay attention to the width of the containers and reverse his judgment. He reasons with single dimensions and does not relate or coordinate them. He has no grasp of the fact that every increase in height is compensated for by a decrease in width.

A second stage is transitional, for, in general, conservation emerges gradually. At this level the child may assume conservation when the liquid is poured into two glasses, or when the differences in the cross-sections or the levels are slight. But if there are more glasses, or the differences in dimensions are increased, the child doubts that the quantity is still the same. He attempts to relate the dimensions of height and width, but in so doing focuses on one or the other and becomes confused. During this stage, however, he does begin to understand the identity of a whole with its halves. Piaget comments that the second stage is not necessarily found in all children.

By the third stage the child assumes conservation for each of the transformations the quantity undergoes. The liquid from one vessel may be poured successively into wider and shallower vessels, or it may be divided into more and more tall, narrow vessels. Whatever the change he observes, the child knows that if the amounts were originally equivalent, they remain equivalent. The protocols Piaget includes suggest that some children are so sure of themselves that it is impossible to fathom the processes involved in their thinking. They simply maintain that the amounts are "the same."

However, by questioning those who hesitate, or who assert nonconservation and quickly correct themselves, Piaget comes to the conclusion that two kinds of reasoning are involved. One, which he terms "logical multiplication of relations," implies the child's ability to compare *simultaneously* the relationships involved when the column of the liquid in one container is both higher and narrower than in the next. The second kind of reasoning involves the idea that the increase in height when the liquid from one container is poured into another is equivalent to the decrease in width. This implies an understanding of proportion and of a unit for comparison.

Conservation of discontinuous quantity

To check on these findings and to explore the development of the understanding of one-one correspondence, Piaget modifies these experiments. In the same glass cylinder as in the previous experiments beads replace the liquid. The child is shown two identical containers. One bead is put in one container and one in the other at the same time. When the two containers are filled to the same level and, of course, contain the same number of beads, one container is emptied into another of different shape, or into several smaller containers, and the questioning proceeds much as in the conservation of liquid experiments. The beads, objects that are familiar to the children, can be compared globally, or perceptually, when they are placed in different containers, or when they are made up into necklaces. But they can also be considered as separate units.

In these experiments, Piaget finds three stages of understanding corresponding to those in the previous experiments. The second, or transitional stage, is particularly revealing. When the perceptual changes are not great, the child asserts conservation, but when the patterns are more drastically altered, he relies once more on the global qualities and maintains that the quantities are different. He may do this even when he has already indicated that if the beads were made into necklaces they would be the same. "There is conservation when the child is thinking of the row of discontinuous elements, and non-conservation when he is thinking of one of the dimensions of the set as a whole" (Piaget, 1952a, p. 30). If the child himself makes a one-one correspondence (dropping two of the beads, one by one, into the containers) he still vacillates. He may move toward the multiplication of relations ("It's round and long here, and round and bigger here"), and then decide that one or the other container has more beads.

In the third stage the children assert conservation immediately and with conviction. To check on the nature of their reasoning, Piaget confronts the children with two sets of beads equivalent in number, arranged in containers markedly different in shape. He asks whether they are the same and how he can find out. The responses of the children indicate that, once they can establish the equivalence by one-one correspondence, they coordinate (multiply) perceptual relationships of height and width. The perceived differences "are measured one against the other, each increases in height and conversely" (Piaget, 1952a, pp. 36–37). The children's thinking has become "operational." Piaget comments on the children's performances:

> When, for instance, Lea says "if I emptied this (P) one into that one (L) or that one (L) into this one (P) they'd be the same" he is expressing the reversibility characteristic of any logical, mathematical operation, and it is this reversibility that makes possible the notion of equalization and decomposition. This is clearly illustrated in the case of Dur who says: "I fill it in my mind and I can see where it comes up to" and "I lay the glass (E) on its side, and then I can see that there's more here (G) because there's some room left" (1952a, p. 37).

One-one correspondence

These experiments do not settle the question of why the equivalence established by one-one correspondence persists for the child in this final stage, but is so illusive for the child in the preceding stage. To investigate this question, Piaget has designed another ingenious series of experiments. Again, the child has an opportunity to match, one by one, the objects in one set with those of another set, in order to establish for himself the fact that the two sets are equivalent in number. But this time Piaget gives the child some additional clues. Perhaps, he reasons, the difficulty in maintaining the equivalence of the two sets when their configuration changed came from the child's inability to bear in mind the match he had made between each of the beads in one set and a bead in the other set. If the match were more obvious, or more functional, the child might retain it more readily. Accordingly he repeats the experiment, using a set of bottles and an equivalent set of glasses, a set of vases and enough flowers to put one flower in each vase, and a set of egg cups with corresponding eggs. The children arrange the objects so that there is a glass for every bottle, a flower for every vase, and so on. The results closely parallel the results for the previous experiments dealing with the conservation of quantity.

In each of the experiments Piaget finds three stages. Initially, the child finds it difficult, if not impossible, to make a one-one correspondence between the two sets of objects. There is little differentiation between the space occupied and quantity. One child of four years and nine months, for example, when confronted with a row of seven egg cups made a row of the same length but containing only four eggs. When asked to put his eggs in the cups he seemed surprised that there were not enough to fill them. The experimenter then made a row of twelve eggs, corresponding in length to the row of seven egg cups. The child indicated that he thought all twelve would go into the egg cups. Even when he had matched the objects in a situation as seemingly obvious as that of the eggs and the egg cups, he doubted the equivalence once the two sets were no longer in alignment.

In the second stage, the child has no difficulty in setting up the objects in a one-one correspondence, but he cannot maintain it when the configuration of the sets is changed. Even when he gives verbal recognition that the objects in the two sets could be returned to their original positions, he still asserts that "there are more" in the configuration that spreads over more space.

In the third stage, the children discover that "any spatial modification in the distribution of the elements can be corrected by an inverse operation" (Piaget, 1952a, p. 56). The information derived from the child's previous observation of the one-one relationship of the objects in the two sets is still accessible to him, and can be used in the face of the perceptual discrepancy.

Further exploration, using pennies and objects, and getting the child to count aloud, reveals approximately the same three levels of understanding. Piaget asserts that neither a one-one exchange, where the child gives the experimenter one penny for each object, nor counting aloud is sufficient to insure equivalence before the child has reached an operational level of thinking.

Having considered situations where the nature of the materials and the opportunities to match objects one to one should serve to bolster and maintain the child's awareness of the equivalence of sets, Piaget next poses tasks in which the child is given fewer cues. In this series of experiments the child is confronted with a figure composed of chips or counters and asked to reproduce it using the same number of chips. The figures vary in complexity, some open, some closed, some familiar, others unfamiliar. In some the shape depends on the number of chips, as in a square, in others, not, as in a circle.

The results parallel those in the preceding experiments. Initially, the child imitates the configuration, but does not quantify. He may, for example, arrange a row of counters so that they are the same length as the model, but use fewer counters. In the case of a familiar form requiring a definite number of counters, he may make a correct copy, but if the figure is unfamiliar, or not dependent on the number of counters, his copy will not be numerically accurate.

In the second stage, the child begins with matching the counters to be used in the copy, on a one-one basis, but if the original figure is then disarranged the child no longer maintains that they have the same number. Piaget uses the responses of this stage to distinguish *qualitative* from *numerical* correspondence, and *intuitive* from *operational* correspondence. In the case of qualitative correspondence the child pays attention to the qualities (angles, for example) of the corresponding elements irrespective of the number of elements in the set. In numerical correspondence the child pays attention to each element, irrespective of its quality. *Intuitive* correspondence as contrasted with *operational* is based entirely on perception and lacks reversibility. When the appearance of the figure changes, the child can no longer recapture the original equivalence of the sets. *Numerical* correspondence, with the possible exception of the first three or four numbers, is essentially operational (Piaget, 1952a, p. 70). Piaget regards this second stage as one in which the correspondence the child makes is not genuinely numerical, but predominately intuitive.

In the third stage, the correspondence becomes operational. Piaget describes how this stage differs from the previous ones, citing an experiment where the child is asked to put out "the same number" of counters to correspond to a row of six objects representing sweets or pennies.

> The child . . . is now capable of considering simultaneously the relationships of length and density, not only when the series to be compared are similar . . . but also when they differ in both length and density. . . . If we consider the total length and density of the rows as two distinct relationships, as the child does before he co-ordinates them, or when he determines the density by the length of the intervals between the elements, we can say that the third stage indicates the completion of the multiplication of these two relationships (1952a, p. 83).

However, Piaget believes, something more than the coordination of relationships is involved here. The elements in the sets are now regarded as units, each equivalent to the others. Accordingly, the same order of enumeration can be applied to each of the sets, and to the intervals between the units.

Other aspects of number

At this point, Piaget recapitulates evidence from his experiments as relating to one-one correspondence and the cardinal number of sets, and simultaneously begins to sketch out some of the aspects of ordination that will be considered in the remainder of *The Child's Conception of Number*. He also discusses the relationship of logical classification to the number concept. Since the experiments from which the conservation tasks in our study have been derived do not deal directly with these aspects, they need not be elaborated here. To ignore them completely, however, would be to present a decidedly one-sided view of Piaget's concept of number. To round out the picture we shall draw on a summary by Lovell:

> . . . for Piaget the concept of number is not based on images or on mere ability to use symbols verbally, but on the formation and systemization in the mind of two operations; classification and seriation. For the concept to form in the mind these two operations must blend, and in order that objects may be both equivalent and yet different, the qualities that are specific to each member of the group must be eliminated so that the homogeneous unit 1 may be formed; for instance the characteristics that distinguish, chairs, jugs, and shells are eliminated and each is regarded as a thing. A practical example will help to make the general position clearer. As the child picks out all blue beads and puts them in a box he comes to think of all blue beads together and eventually forms the concept of "class of all blue objects." By sorting other materials he can likewise form the concept of other classes; the concept of a class, or the mental operation of classifying, is an internalized version of grouping together objects as similar. Again, in his activities involving seriation he puts bricks in order of length from, say, left to right. From this kind of action he derives the concept of relations. The number system is the union of classification and ordering, for the idea of the number 8, say, depends upon the child grouping in his mind eight objects to form a class, and upon placing 8 between 7 and 9; that is, in relation (1961, p. 51).

Related Studies

A considerable number of studies, some conducted by Piaget and his colleagues at Geneva, others by researchers in England, Canada, and more recently the United States, have used Piaget's theories regarding the development of the concept of number as their point of departure. Those appearing in the literature before and during 1961 have been well reviewed by Flavell (1963, pp. 358–363, 381–388), and our consideration of them can be limited in detail.

To a greater or lesser extent all of these studies have addressed themselves to four main questions. First, are the stages of development described by Piaget identifiable in other populations? Second (and this is clearly related to the first), within any given stage are the relationships among underlying abilities similar to those set forth in the theory? Third, how is attainment of a particular level of thought (operational as opposed to intuitive, for example) related to progress in intellectual development as measured in other ways? Fourth, to what extent is progress from one level of thought to another impeded or facilitated by various kinds of experience, or, more specifically, can training accelerate the transition?

Validity of the stages

In general, studies that have replicated Piaget's experiments dealing with the conservation of quantity and number have tended to support his findings regarding the sequence of stages. A stage of pervasive nonconservation is followed by one in which the child may vacillate between conserving and nonconserving responses. At this point conservation appears to be somewhat dependent on the nature and extent of the observed transformations. Finally, the child's concepts of quantity and number become stable, and he is no longer deceived by appearances. However, a particular child may attain conservation in one kind of task and not reveal it in another related task.

What was probably the first attempt to validate Piaget's findings in regard to number concepts with American children was a study by Estes (1956). She reported "no evidence" to support his theory of stages in their acquisition. The work of later investigators suggests that Estes' methods may have influenced her results.

Dodwell (1960) replicated five of Piaget's experiments, in "fairly standardized" form. The subjects were children in kindergarten through second grade, ranging in age from five to ten years. The first three tests involved conservation. In one, the child compared the number of two sets of beads, for which he had already established the equivalence, after they were placed in beakers of varying shapes. In another, eggs and egg cups were used, and in a third, poker chips. The three stages of thought were clearly distinguishable, but there were marked variations from task to task. Eighty per cent of the children at age five years and ten months showed operational thinking when dealing with the eggs and egg cups, but none of the children of that age conserved in the experiment with the chips (where the one-one correspondence was least obvious) and 80 per cent conserved in the experiment with the beads (where they had established the correspondence themselves).

Dodwell's study also included tests of seriation and cardination-ordination which showed even less clear age trends than the conservation tasks. In the seriation task the child matched dolls and canes of graded sizes. After they had been arranged in order, the dolls were spread out and the child questioned as to which cane went with which doll, and how he knew. The cardination and ordination task involved a stair constructed from blocks. The child had to indicate the number of blocks needed for each succeeding step, and the number of steps preceding it. In a later reanalysis of the data Dodwell (1961) noted that factors other than the difficulty of the tasks apparently affected the test, and that even with the seriation task omitted, it was, at best a "quasi-scale." He concluded that "the pattern of development of number concepts does not follow the sequence described by Piaget with great regularity" (p. 36).

Elkind, using American subjects, repeated a number of Piaget's experiments related to the conservation of quantity. One study (Elkind, 1961b) included youngsters ranging in age from four through seven, and involved experiments with sticks, beads, and liquid. Success in comparing quantities increased significantly with age. The experiment with the liquid was the most difficult. Statistical analysis of the interaction of age and type of quantity indicated that, while the order of difficulty of the types was the same at each age, differences in difficulty decreased with age.

In another study Elkind (1961a) tested children from kindergarten through sixth grade for their abilities in conserving mass, weight, and volume. The results approximated Piaget's findings. Children aged five and six differed significantly from those who were seven or older in their ability to conserve mass (in this case, identical clay balls, one of which was transformed to a "hot dog" in shape).

Lovell (Lovell & Ogilvie, 1960), who, with his colleagues, has carried on a number of replication studies, repeated the experiment involving conservation of substance. This study used plasticene balls. The questions were standardized but a flexible approach was maintained. The youngest children, pupils in English junior schools, were seven years old. The investigators found strong support for the three stages of thinking proposed by Piaget, but also noted that the stages were not clear-cut.

Wohlwill (1960), translating Piaget's theory of the development of the number concept into behavior theory terms, and using a matching rather than a verbal technique, designed a series of tasks paralleling Piaget's number experiments. He tested Swiss children, ranging in age from four to seven, and found that the responses could be categorized into three stages. He indicates that the results demonstrate the existence of a relatively uniform developmental sequence in the area of number, confirming the theoretical views of Piaget.

Hood studied the development of number in normal, educationally subnormal,[1] and mentally defective English children. He used Piaget's clinical method, and included, among others, tasks involving the conservation of an amount of liquid, and of sets of chips, as well as sets of functionally related objects. He comments:

> A teacher relying on chronological age grouping and making due allowance for exceptional cases, could feel reasonably sure that a large majority of her under-fives would have little appreciation of pre-number concepts, that those above seven could usually be counted on to approach full understanding, but that in the two year period from five to seven no assumption should be made (Hood, 1962, p. 276).

Results from the retarded subjects indicated that prenumber concepts tend to mature as all-around mental capacity increases.

Two other English studies of subnormal individuals tend to support Piaget's notion of stages in the development of number concepts. Mannix (1960) interviewed educationally subnormal children ranging

---

[1] The term *educationally subnormal* refers to pupils who for reasons of limited ability or other conditions resulting in educational retardation require some form of specialized education.

in chronological age from five years to eight years and eleven months. The mental age at which children entered the stage of concrete operations varied widely from child to child. However, no child with a mental age of less than six years and eight months performed at the level of concrete operations in all the tests. No child with a mental age of more than six years and five months was at the preoperational stage in all the tests.

Woodward (1961) studied retarded children and adults. The median IQ (WAIS) for the adult group, who had a mean chronological age of 19 years, was 49.5. The children with a mean chronological age of 12 years had a median IQ (Binet) of 34. Their responses resembled those of normal children aged four to seven years. Most subjects performed consistently either at the concrete operational stage or at the intuitive level for all the problems. A transitional stage also appeared.

Studies such as these tend to refute the mistaken conception that the stages of intellectual development posed by Piaget are necessarily bound to chronological age. In discussing stages, Piaget often uses the phrase "on the average," suggesting that variation is to be expected, but the protocols with which he illustrates a particular stage usually come from children representing such a narrow age range as to invoke confusion. Furthermore, readers unfamiliar with the breadth of investigations carried on by Piaget's collaborators may not know that his experiments have been effectively used in the diagnosis of mental retardation (Inhelder, 1963).

Accumulating evidence also suggests that in a general way the sequence of development of number concepts is similar among populations with rather diverse backgrounds. Flavell (1963) reports that Hyde found that Arab, Hindu, and Somali school children living in Aden responded much as had Piaget's subjects. Price-Williams (1961) interviewed illiterate West African children, using classic experiments to test the conservation of continuous and discontinuous quantities. His results support the progression of comprehension suggested by Piaget. Reports from Japan (Noro, 1961) indicate that similar stages are found among the Japanese children, although one article (Fujinaga, Saiga, & Hosoya, 1963) suggests that "too much attention is paid to the natural sequence of developmental stages and not enough to the role of learning." A negative note comes also from Peking,

China (Cheng & Lee, 1964), where the results of "an experiment" are said to run contrary to the contention of the "bourgeois scholar Piaget" that "children's conception of number is completely determined by age."

On the whole, however, the bulk of the replication studies in the literature supports the notion that the child's ability to conserve quantity and number is arrived at gradually, and that a period of nonconservation, or perceptual domination, is followed by a transitional stage, before conservation becomes pervasive. This conclusion, so far as we were able to determine from our review of the literature, comes almost without exception from studies involving children of different ages. Inhelder (Tanner & Inhelder, 1953) indicates that some children have been studied longitudinally, but the results are not presently available.

To a considerable extent, the question of whether the major stages in the development of the concept of number will be revealed when non-Swiss children are confronted with Piaget's experiments has become a dead issue. Much more viable is the question of whether the relationships among the abilities that he asserts are characteristic of a particular stage can be verified.

Relationships among abilities within stages

Piaget, as Flavell puts it, has "a penchant for symmetry and neatness of classification" (1963, p. 38). An unwary reader may find himself persuaded that the symmetry in the theory exists in fact. For example, the concept of number is seen as a synthesis of the ability to classify objects on the basis of likenesses and to order them on the basis of differences. The notion of a unit of measurement emerges as the child on the one hand mentally breaks up a configuration, and, on the other, rearranges its parts. In turn, the concept of a unit parallels the emerging ability to deal simultaneously with two relationships. But Piaget's work seldom reveals whether the symmetry implicit in his theory is to be found in the actual thinking of an individual child. Accordingly, one might expect to find a number of studies testing whether the abilities Piaget attributes to a given stage correlate as closely as he suggests.

Certain facets of the theory must be borne in mind if its adequacy is to be tested appropriately. First, the synthesis, or drawing together,

of two or more abilities (Piaget would probably use the term structures) into a new and more effective ability, presumably represents
the attainment of one stage and the starting point of the next (Inhelder, 1962). The extent to which an investigator finds the abilities
to be related should accordingly vary considerably depending on the
age range in his population. If it happens to be such as to include only
children who have already attained a given level the results should
vary considerably from those obtained when the abilities are being
formed.

Secondly, the theory specifies that abilities during the period of
their formation are not applied equally well to all kinds of tasks. For
example, the ability to conserve the weight of an object typically lags
a year or two behind the ability to conserve its substance. This suggests that the investigator needs to be sure that the tasks he uses to
demonstrate particular abilities or structures do not differ in the level
of their difficulty.

Despite these problems, studies which attempt to establish that
the relationships hypothesized by Piaget exist in fact, have not only
theoretical but practical value. The instruction provided children in
school could obviously be facilitated if more were known of the
abilities essential to mastery of certain key concepts.

To date, only a limited number of studies have dealt with the relationship among abilities or structures at any given level. The conclusions to be drawn are not too clear. Lunzer's (1960) statement still
holds: "It is by no means certain that because some relations are
fundamental to the *logical* analysis of mathematical properties, these
same relations underlie the *psychological* evolution of the recognition
of these properties" (p. 201).

Dodwell (1960) in his previously mentioned study involving kindergarten, first-, and second-grade children, found that some of the children could deal operationally with cardinal-ordinal properties before
they could deal with either classes or series separately. Further, if
they could deal with classes and series separately, it was not necessarily true that they could deal with numbers as constructs combining
ordinal and cardinal relations.

In a later study Dodwell (1962) investigated the relationships between developing concepts of number and quality and the ability to
handle classification problems. In this study, the questioning related

to number was separated in time from that related to classification and the materials used were presented in random order, thus avoiding whatever contamination might result from a set to respond in a particular way. Most of the correlations between the answers to the classification problems and the items on the number tests were low and not significant. Dodwell suggests that children typically receive considerable instruction in the development of number concepts but little, if any, in the nature of hierarchical classifications.

Lovell and Ogilvie (1960) in the previously cited study of the conservation of substance attempted to determine whether children who conserved also used kinds of logical abilities that Piaget had described as essential. After the main experiment had established which children were conservers, several auxiliary experiments were done to test out the thinking of those who had not conserved or appeared to be in a transitional stage. The results led the investigators to question whether the reversibility, coordinated relations and identity operations described by Piaget as essential to conservation were so in fact. They found six nonconservers who were capable of considering two dimensions in compensatory fashion when the exigencies of the experiment forced them to do so. Also they found some children who gave evidence of reversibility (defined as acknowledging that the balls of clay "were the same before") who did not conserve. One suspects that Piaget might criticize both their experimental techniques and their definitions, but the study is illustrative of needed experimentation.

Several more recent studies, dealing with the conservation of weight and volume, may also be cited as typical investigations of the intricate network of relationships postulated by Piaget. The child, according to Piaget, does not achieve the conservation of weight until a year or so after he is able to conserve substance, quantity, or number. At this time he is presumably more firmly established in the stage of operational thinking, less erratic in his behavior generally, and more amenable to testing. Accordingly, one might anticipate more reliable and valid results in experiments dealing with the ability to conserve weight than in those dealing with the conservation of number or quantity.

Piaget maintains that just as the ability to conserve number is in part contingent on the ability to order objects according to their size, so the ability to conserve weight is paralleled by the ability to place objects in series, according to their weight. Further involved in seriation is the ability to recognize transitivity, that is, the ability to coordinate a series of observed relationships when three or more objects are compared in some way. (If object A is greater in weight than object B, and object B than object C, then one knows that A is greater than C without making direct comparison of the two.)

Lovell and Ogilvie (1961) found that most of the children in an English junior school (ages not given but probably ranging from seven years up) who conserved weight could perform the logical operation of transitivity in relation to weight. But many nonconservers could also do so. Smedslund (1961b), working with Norwegian subjects ranging in age from five years and six months to seven years, used a technique that offered each child four different opportunities to conserve and also to perform the transitivity operation. His results differed strikingly from those of Lovell and Ogilvie in that there was little association between the two abilities. Chittenden (1964), with American subjects, ages six to eleven, found parallel sequences for the conservation of weight and the transitivity operation. However, he did not find that seriation comparisons based on weight were more difficult than those based on size.

Differences in the nature of the tasks provided and differences in the age groups studied may account for discrepant results in these and similar studies. Or it may be the two abilities are indeed related, as Piaget suggests, but that educational and other experiences have tended to facilitate the development of one and not the other.

Several investigators have speculated that a kind of general intellectual ability underlies each of the stages of intellectual development described by Piaget. Whiteman (1964), for example, has proposed that Piaget's theory of behavioral consistency at a given developmental stage (his notion of operation) needs further examination from the view of other psychological theories. Using a factor analytic approach, a wide variety of tests designed to call on operational thought would be given to a large group of children, and the consistencies from test to test examined. Or, taking the tack of "learning set," the effects on individual children of varied conservation experiences could be appraised to see to what extent the underlying consistency of operational thought might arise out of these.

So far little work of this sort has been reported. Beard (1960) used factor analysis to examine the results when a concept test involving seven categories, several clearly drawn from Piaget's work, was individually administered to sixty English six- and seven-year-olds. The children also took the Terman-Merrill Test. The first factor appeared to be related to general verbal ability. Another factor derived mainly from items dealing with the child's conception of the world and taking of another's point of view, suggesting Piaget's "emergence from ego-centric notions." Another factor was concerned with quantity. Elkind (1961b), in his study testing the conservation of four- to seven-year-olds with three different kinds of materials, reported high intercorrelations among the scores and interpreted this as supporting Piaget's assumption of a common conceptualizing ability.

On the whole, the presently available evidence regarding the relationships among the abilities or structures at any given stage of development can hardly be regarded as satisfactory. The theory, as Lunzer (1960) has suggested, may be too logical to represent psychological reality. Or the methods so far designed to test the theory may be inept. Small wonder that some psychologists and some educators continue to question whether investigations based on the theory will yield much more information about intellectual development than is already available from the use of other measures.

Performance on Piaget tasks and other measures of mental ability

In considering the relationships that one might reasonably expect to find between children's performance in Piaget's tests of their numerical and logical abilities, and their performance in the kinds of tasks that go to make up the more usual tests of intelligence, two points are important.

First, to the extent that Piaget's tasks are tests of concept formation, the correlations with intelligence are likely to be low. In this connection Vinacke comments on

> the apparently low correlation of "concept test" scores with intelligence-test scores and their relatively high correlation with training experience, of which one important component seems to be vocabulary. Whether the latter relationship depends upon chronological age or upon amount and kind of training has not been clearly worked out (1952, p. 120).

Second, Piaget's conception of intelligence differs in important respects from the psychometric notions that dominate most of the tests currently in use. As Hunt (1961) has suggested, Piaget's theory implies a natural, ordinal scale of intelligence that contrasts in important ways with the view of a more or less fixed IQ.

It may be that these differing views are not readily reconcilable. But until the fact has been established one might expect to find many studies exploring the possible relationships between the two views of intelligence. To date it seems to have been more customary for those who have carried on Piaget experimentation to report simply that their subjects were selected from a middle class school population, or had measured IQ's falling within a specified range. A few of the studies dealing with conservation also report other measures.

Beard (1960) indicates that performance on his concept test, consisting in part of Piaget tasks, correlates .38 with MA (Terman-Merrill). The correlation with CA was .16. The latter correlation resulted in part from the very narrow age range, but Beard concludes that "development in concept formation depends more on increase in mental age than chronological age, contrary to what Piaget usually implies in his discussion of stages" (p. 21).

Elkind (1961b) in his study of quantitative thinking, replicating Piaget's experiments with sticks, liquids, and beads, found significant correlations with some of the WISC subtests (Information .47, Arithmetic .35, Picture Arrangement .55, Object Assembly .38, Coding .42). Correlation with the full scale IQ was .43, with verbal performance, .47.

Dodwell (1961) in a study using a number concept test based on Piaget tasks compared rural and urban children ages five through ten. He found no significant differences in performance between rural and urban groups, as a whole, nor between IQ levels, but a highly significant interaction between IQ and urban-rural residence. This seemed to be due to a large difference in favor of the urban group for the average IQ's and in favor of the rural group for the low IQ's. In a later study (1962) testing the children's ability to make logical classifications, he noted a tendency for older and brighter children to do better than others. The correlation with IQ was .34.

Two British studies, in which children with subnormal intelligence were included, report correlations between performance on Piaget experiments dealing with number, and other measures of mental ability. Mannix (1960), using a small group of children with MA's from five to eleven, used Guttman's technique of scalogram analysis and obtained rank order correlations of scaled test responses with mental age of .61, and with chronological age of .52. Hood (1962) found that none of the children with an MA (Terman-Merrill) of less than five years conserved. An MA of five to six marked the point at which some began to conserve, while those who had an MA of eight to nine or better were clearly conserving.

Perhaps the safest generalization to be made from current evidence regarding the relationship between performance on Piaget tasks and mental ability as measured on other tests is that to some extent brightness pays off. The crucial element may be verbal ability. Or it may be an ability to tune in readily to an adult way of organizing. Conceivably, unusual abilities in handling spatial relationships may contribute at an early age. It is not yet possible to appraise the role played by the child's "equipment" as a biological entity, in contrast to the role played by the nature of his encounter with his environment. Nor can we assess the adequacy of what Hunt (1961) terms the "match" between the two.

The role of experience

On several occasions Piaget and his collaborators have indicated their awareness that the age at which a child attains conservation is in part a function of the experiences he has had (Inhelder & Piaget, 1958, p. 337; Tanner & Inhelder, 1953, p. 85). Piaget has remarked that "experience is always necessary for intellectual development" and has specified the importance of physical activity and social interactions as ingredients of experience (1964, p. 31). Despite this, and despite his elaboration of his equilibration theory, Piaget has, in Flavell's terms, "shed little empirical hard-fact light on precisely how [the cognitive structures he demonstrates] work their way into the child's cognitive life" (1963, p. 370).

Flavell (1963) describes two strategies for finding out how conservation and other Piagetian concepts develop. One strategy would involve direct observation of the child's day-to-day encounters with his environment. Flavell notes that a model for such a strategy might be the ecological studies of Barker and Wright (1951, 1955). Piaget's (1952b, 1954, 1962) observational studies of his own three children in infancy and early childhood might also serve, as could Navarra's (1955) study of his child's acquisition of certain scientific concepts.

Flavell writes that no such direct observational studies have been undertaken, nor have we been able to locate any. However, portions of Churchill's (1961) *Counting and Measuring,* a volume based in large part on Piagetian theory, strongly suggest that she derived many of her ideas from observation, possibly informal, of the cognitive activity of children during their play.

Churchill (1958a, 1958b) was one of the first researchers to attempt to influence children's number concepts through the use of an experimental training procedure. Her experimental group made considerable gains. However, as Flavell comments, "the training procedure and the behavior it was to affect were too global and heterogeneous to permit any definite conclusion as to just what experience did and did not influence precisely what numerical skills" (1963, p. 371). Conceivably, Churchill's techniques were effective simply because they provided a variety of different kinds of experience.

As a training study, Churchill's work (1958a, 1958b) represents Flavell's second strategy for determining how Piagetian concepts are formed. The experimenter begins with an analysis of the specific elements or skills that seem likely to be involved in a particular concept. Then, he identifies a group of children who are clearly not yet in possession of the concept at issue, divides them into experimental and control groups, and systematically tries out various techniques for building the missing elements into their repertoire of responses. The techniques chosen depend on whatever theory about the nature of human learning the experimenter holds. Eventually, the experimental and control groups are again tested for the concept. If the experimenter has isolated an essential element of the concept, and if his training technique is appropriate, the experimental groups should be superior to the control groups (unless by some unfortunate chance the controls by virtue of some unknown interaction of experience and maturation have also moved ahead). If the experimental groups show no improvement, the researcher may attempt to isolate new elements, or underlying skills, or devise new training techniques, or he may decide to test out new combinations of these.

The critical variable often turns out to be age, particularly when young children are involved. Thus, an experimental group with a mean age of six years may appear completely resistant to training techniques that are immediately effective with children a year older.

Piaget is said to have remarked that whenever you tell Americans about some process of development their immediate question is "How can you accelerate it?" In fairness, strategy that attempts to unravel a developmental process by providing training prior to the time when a concept would "normally" appear, does not necessarily imply the judgment that the concept *ought* to be taught earlier. On the other hand, the incredulous expression of the experimental psychologist who discovers that his own otherwise intelligent five-year-old does not conserve, and the sometimes grim determination with which he sets about correcting this condition bear witness to the fact that some American psychologists do have some interest in speeding up the process of cognitive development.

Taken as a whole, the experimental studies that have attempted to accelerate the understanding of conservation in young children who were clearly nonconservers have been rather unsuccessful. On the other hand, they do reveal the complexity of the cognitive processes that are involved in the concept.

Flavell (1963) reviews the major early studies. Beilin and Franklin (1962), Wohlwill and Lowe (1962), Harker (1960), Smedslund (1961b, 1961c, 1961d, 1961e, 1961f), and Bruner (1964) describe some of the more recent experiments. We shall limit our discussion here to consideration of the training techniques that have been used and their general effectiveness. In the latter connection, it is well to remember Piaget's (1964) caution that the ultimate test of an experimental procedure's effectiveness is to be found in the duration and generalization of the concept. Is there evidence of the learning two weeks or a month later? Does it transfer to situations other than those encountered in the psychological laboratory?

So far as the conservation of the number of objects in a set is concerned, the most obvious way to teach the child is to have him count before and after the objects are rearranged. If he does this often enough, with appropriate reinforcement to help him recognize that the correct answer is the same number regardless of the arrangement, one would expect him to shift eventually to conservation.

(Piaget contends, on the other hand, that such counting is meaningless, except perhaps in the case of the smallest numbers, until the child has spontaneously arrived at conservation.) Another related training technique is to demonstrate to the child that either adding objects or subtracting objects does indeed change the number. A third technique focuses more directly on the perceptual aspects by giving the child opportunities to observe that a particular set of objects may be extended or compressed in space without changing its number. Wohlwill and Lowe (1962) used all these techniques, setting up a matching procedure to avoid the complexities induced by verbal techniques. When they used nonverbal techniques for measuring conservation, the experimental groups did show improvement, but on the usual verbal measures, the training had no effect.

Smedslund (1961b) approached the problem of the conservation of weight in somewhat similar fashion, with equally unproductive results. In a later experiment (1961c) he tested Piaget's notion that the concept of conservation has to be spontaneously constructed by the child himself, if it is to have any degree of permanence. He worked with two groups of children, one of which had been "taught" to conserve weight in the experimental situation, and another in which the children were already conserving, at the time the study began. As a test of the stability of the children's concepts of conservation, Smedslund confronted each of them with two balls of plasticene that weighed the same when placed on the balance scale. He then changed the shape of one of the balls, and surreptitiously removed some of the plasticene while he was getting the child's prediction as to whether it would weigh the same as the unaltered ball. The children who had supposedly "learned" to conserve in the experimental training quickly reverted to nonconservation. But those who had been conserving from the beginning were not so easily taken in. They tended to protest that something had happened; if the balls had weighed the same originally, they should continue to despite changes in appearance.

In a later study dealing with the conservation of substance, Smedslund (1961e, 1961f) systematically introduced cognitive conflict into the experiment. He would, for example, stretch out a piece of the plasticene, a procedure which a particular child might take as evidence of increase in the amount. But he would also remove a portion, which the same child might expect to reduce the quantity. On the whole, children who went through the cognitive conflict procedures, receiving no external reinforcement, did better on the posttest than their counterparts who received no training.

Although Smedslund's work provides extremely interesting evidence that conservation represents a kind of synthesis of cognitive experience that cannot be arrived at by simply going through a series of exercises, it doesn't say much about how this takes place with the child who never happens to turn up in a psychological experiment. As Wohlwill says, "There must be something in the normal process of development that takes the place of this experience. . . . In general it seems to me implausible to suppose that a child is normally exposed to that much cognitive dissonance, . . . in the kindergarten or first grade period during which these things seem to develop 'spontaneously'" (1964, p. 97).

Wohlwill takes the view that it is probably impossible to design experiences that will shift a child who is at the height of a perceptually dominated stage to a different kind of reasoning. Rather, as the "language and other mediational processes such as observing responses" develop, the perceptual approach sloughs off (1964, p. 98). Zimles (1963) holds a similar view.

More recent studies seem to be shifting away from study of the processes involved in conservation *per se* toward consideration of related perceptual and language factors. For example, Bruner (1964) reports an experiment derived from the technique used by Piaget to study the conservation of an amount of liquid. Nine glasses, varying in three degrees of diameter and three degrees of height are arranged in a matrix in front of a child. After the child has described how the rows are alike and how they differ, the glasses are scrambled, and the child is asked to rebuild the matrix. Five-, six-, and seven-year-olds have no difficulty with this part of the experiment. But when one glass is transposed from one side of the matrix to the other, and the child is asked to reconstruct the matrix, leaving the one glass in its new position, difficulty arises. The younger children in the study appeared to be dominated by the picture of the original matrix, some even building over the transposed glass. The seven-year-olds, on the other hand, saw the relation of place and size as a problem to be reasoned out and talked out their solutions. Bruner notes that their language could be classified in three different linguistic modes. One was dimensional, "That one is higher, and that one shorter." Another was global, "That one is bigger, and that one little." This could be used for any diameter. A third was confounded. Here the child used a dimensional term for one end of the continuum and a global term for the other, "That one is tall, and that one little." Children using the confounded descriptions had the most difficulty with the transposition task, although the use of language bore no relation to success in copying the original matrix.

Bruner suggests that improvement in language might help the child in solving a problem such as this. He further proposes that language might serve as a kind of prop to help the child overcome the pull of his visual perceptions. He reports an experiment conducted by Frank. After doing the classic conservation tests involving the liquid in beakers of various sizes, Frank introduced a screen. The child could see the original equivalence of the water in two beakers of identical appearance, but when the water was poured from one of these into a beaker of different size, the third beaker (but not the pouring process) was screened from the child's view. At this point the experimenter asked whether the amount in the third beaker would be more or the same. The number of correct judgments greatly increased. However, when the screen was removed, all the four-year-olds changed their minds. But 70 per cent of the five-years-olds stuck with their conserving responses. This was in marked contrast to the 20 per cent who had conserved on the pretest.

Brison (1964) reports an experiment that appears to combine elements from some of those already described here, while adding some new features. In this experiment, children who had demonstrated that they could not conserve in the classic tests were divided into small groups. To each of these small groups was added a child who had indicated in the pretest that he was transitional, or vacillating, in conservation. At this point fruit juice was introduced, in *unequal* amounts, to be shared as it was poured into vessels of varying sizes. The trick, it appears, was for the child to keep his mind firmly on the problem of getting the most juice for himself, something that one five-year-old reportedly accomplished, as he put it, by "remembering it in my head." In any event, children who participated in the experiment showed enough gains on posttests of conservation to warrant further experimentation.

Beilin (1964), who in an early study (Beilin & Franklin, 1962) found that instruction affected first graders' conservation of length but not area, has recently conducted an experiment designed to analyze perceptual-cognitive conflict in this kind of conservation problem. An electrically lighted visual pattern board provides a situation analogous to an early Piaget experiment. In this experiment the child is confronted with two model farms on which an equal number of identical barns can be variously arranged on the meadows in order to test whether the child believes there may be more "grass for the cow to eat" when the barns are spaced apart than when they are together. Beilin's apparatus permits the child to be confronted simultaneously with two geometric figures composed of lighted squares. He is asked to judge whether the areas in the two figures are equal or unequal. In this experiment each child responded to three series of comparisons: *equality*, where the areas of the two figures were equal and the pattern arrangements congruent; *inequality*, where one figure had one or more squares more or less than the other; *quasiconservation*, where the areas of the two figures were equal but one was so arranged as to appear perceptually different from the other. In some of the comparisons the basic figures were made up from four squares, in others from nine squares. The children's judgments were scored as to their correctness (areas of the figures the same or not the same) in each of the three series and, additionally, in the inequality series, for correctness of judgment as to which figure had more or less area. This judgment is termed a "categorical judgment."

As might be anticipated on the basis of Piaget's theory, the youngest (kindergarten) children had a high level of performance in perceptual judgment (based on the equality and inequality series). First and second graders were nearly perfect in the same judgments. But the categorical judgment presented a different picture, with the percentage of accuracy dropping to as low as 13.3 per cent (for figures involving nine squares) in kindergarten, and improving steadily to third grade where it was 83 per cent. Quasi-conservation responses were even more difficult, with the percentage of correct responses (for the nine square figures) ranging from 0 in kindergarten to 38 per cent by fourth grade.

So far as learning during the experiment was concerned, performance tended to have an all-or-none characteristic. Those who began responding incorrectly were still incorrect at the end of a series of ten presentations.

Beilin questioned the children in the quasi-conservation series as to how they knew whether the figures were the same or different, and then made a content analysis of their responses. According to Piaget's theory, there are two ways in which children may "measure" area in this sort of problem. One (iterative) is to count the squares, the other (superpositional) involves mentally placing one figure over the other and judging whether the excess parts equal the missing ones. The children's responses indicated that they tended to use the first method for the four square figures, the second for the nine square figures. This suggests a principle of "cognitive efficiency" in which the thought process used is the one that will require the least time and effort for processing the sensory data.

Beilin's discussion of the results is noteworthy for its exploration of the variety of ways a child may view the problems confronting him in an experiment such as this, and the reasons that may lie behind his errors in judgment. He contrasts the difficulties involved in the judgments "larger" and "smaller" ("more" and "less") with those in "same" and "different." Like Bruner (1964), he notes that incorrect labeling may be a problem. Some children, for example, seem to understand when to apply the term "more," but not "less." They may, however, know the term "littler." On the other hand, many children who could not label correctly also revealed that they had no grasp of the logical necessity for judgment of "less" for a second figure, if the first figure of a pair had been labeled "more."

It seems clear from current experimentation that the question of just what is involved in the transition from nonconservation to conservation, or from thought that is predominately perceptual and intuitive to thought that is more conceptual and logical, or, in Piaget's terms, "operational," is far from settled. Most of the evidence seems to weigh against the possibility that the transition can be accelerated by any short term manipulation. What might be accomplished by more pervasive intervention also remains an open question. But it may be well to bear in mind the fact that the ability to conserve represents only one dimension of the child's developing intellectual power. There is, as Wohlwill points out, a possibility of "accelerating the process of cognitive development with respect to one particular concept at the expense of the breadth or generality of learning or transfer to other later concepts" (1964, p. 100).

Despite the current spate of experimentation related to conservation, it seems unlikely that either psychology or education is prepared to launch any large scale attempt at acceleration. But better understanding of the ways the child does acquire the concept of conservation offers considerable promise for more effective instruction of children during the early childhood years. It is with this possibility that our studies have been concerned.

The Present Investigation

The primary question to which our studies were directed had to do with the validity of the stages of thought described by Piaget. The gathering of longitudinal as well as cross-sectional data permits a kind of perspective heretofore largely lacking.

The cognitive ability in the foreground of these studies has been that involved in understanding the principle of conservation, particularly as it applies to quantity and number. But to the extent that it is possible to infer a child's ability to classify from his performance in predicting and explaining the floating and sinking behavior of objects, the studies have dealt with this additional ability. Also at issue has been the relationship between the ability to conserve and the abilities measured in the more traditional tests of mental ability and academic achievement.

The question of the contribution of experience to progress in conservation has been of major concern. The data have accordingly been drawn from two populations that, by virtue of their home backgrounds, can be assumed to have very different preschool experiences.

In the following chapters the results from our studies are presented. After describing our methods and procedures in Chapter 3, we turn to the cross-sectional study in Chapter 4; move on to the longitudinal study in Chapter 5. Then we consider the results related to children's views on the floating and sinking of objects in Chapter 6.

□ CHAPTER 3

Methods and procedures

IN 1960 WHEN the details of the cross-sectional and longitudinal studies were planned, the renaissance of interest in Piaget among psychologists had already begun. Bruner's provocative volume *The Process of Education* (1960), drawing on certain aspects of Piaget theory, was exciting the interest of educators.

Our pilot study, and the senior investigator's explorations with teachers and parents, confirmed the notion that the transition from intuitive or "preoperational" to "operational" thought constitutes an important landmark in the child's ability to learn from adult instruction. As Bruner (1960, pp. 34–35) put it:

> What is principally lacking at this stage of development is what the Geneva school has called the concept of reversibility. When the shape of an object is changed, as when one changes the shape of a ball of plasticene, the preoperational child cannot grasp the idea that it can be brought back readily to its original state. Because of this fundamental lack the child cannot understand certain fundamental ideas that lie at the basis of mathematics and physics—the mathematical idea that one conserves quantity even when one partitions a set of things into subgroups, or the physical idea that one conserves mass and weight even though one transforms the shape of an object. *It goes without saying that teachers are severely limited in transmitting concepts to a child at this stage, even in a highly intuitive manner.* [Italics supplied.]

When is it reasonable for a teacher to expect that the children with whom she works have developed thought processes sufficiently like her own that they can deal with ideas in similar fashion? Piaget theory (Inhelder, 1962) sets seven as a pivotal age between the long process of "elaboration" of mental operations and the equally long process of "structuration." Not until about seven is "reversibility" attained and understanding of the principle of the conservation of matter possible. The major concern of this study was to establish some notion of the extent of such understanding among children from five to eight years.

Related to this was the question of whether children who displayed such understanding would differ from those who did not, on measures of school achievement and on other measures of intellectual functioning. Also, would they think in different ways about the experiences that might be included in the elementary science aspects of the curriculum? Further, would children who "conserved" at earlier ages show patterns of thinking persistently different from other children?

These were the questions that guided the selection of material for the interviews and of the other tests to be included.

The Interview

Construction of the interview schedule

Anyone undertaking Piaget-inspired research is immediately confronted with certain dilemmas. Which of the many experiments that Piaget has reported shall he replicate? How many experiments are necessary to demonstrate that a child has achieved reversibility in his thinking, or that he does or does not conserve? Shall he follow the clinical method precisely as described by Piaget, or shall he attempt to standardize the demonstrations and questions? If he chooses the latter, will he no longer be investigating Piaget (Braine, 1962)?

The choice of experiments for this study was made after an initial exploration with children of ideas derived from Piaget's *The Child's Conception of the World* (1951b) and *The Child's Conception of Physical Causality* (1951a), volumes presenting research of the late 1920's. However, the more recent *Le développement des quantités chez l'enfant* (1941) and *The Child's Conception of Number* (1952a) together with Piaget and Inhelder's contributions to *Discussions on Child Development* (1953) provided the theoretical background for the study, and led to the selection of one experiment involving the conservation of a given number of objects, and another involving a given amount of liquid. These experiments, approximately in the form described below, were tried out with a group of 25 five- to eight-year-olds of mixed socioeconomic backgrounds before the major study was undertaken.

As the detailed description of the tasks below indicates, each child had five opportunities to indicate that he could conserve and three opportunities for explanation. While this number of responses is small in comparison to the number elicited in a typical Piaget interview where all suspected answers are probed, several considerations, including the practical one of time, weighed against more extensive experimentation.

It seemed particularly important to allow considerable opportunity for each child to understand the intent of the experimenter's questions to make sure that he had the language available for an adequate response. Consequently each experiment was preceded by a training session in which a pattern of correct responses was established. Varying the number of objects, or the amount of liquid to be compared, the experimenter induced the child's use of the terms "the same," "more than," or "less than." The crucial question posed when the amounts involved were identical but the configurations had been altered could then be put as "What about now?" This procedure considerably reduced the number of instances where it was necessary to ask a cue-laden question such as, "Is there more here, or more here, or are they the same?"

Experiments

The conservation experiments, always presented in the same order (and illustrated in Figure 3–1) were as follows:

1. Conservation of number

Task A. During training the child compares eight yellow cubes with eleven red ones, and adds yellow cubes to make the rows the same, then compares the rows with one red removed, one red added, two yellows removed, two added, and so on. For the experiment, the red blocks are bunched and the child is asked "What about now?" If

Figure 3-1. Conversation Tasks

Task A

TRAINING:

E: *Are there just as many yellow blocks as red blocks? You take some more and make it so there are just as many.*

After child does so (or is assisted in doing so), E removes 1 red, asks *What about now?* and, if necessary, *Are there just as many red ones as yellow ones? Are there more yellow ones?* Continues removing 2 yellows, returning 2 yellows, etc.

Test 1:

E: *What about now?*

Test 2:

E: *What about now?*

Test 3:

E: *Why do you think so?*

Task B

COUNTING:

E: *Can you count? Can you find out how many blocks there are? You count them.* (Assist as necessary.)

E: *So how many blocks are there?*

E: *How many now? (Can you tell without counting?)*

E: *How many now?*

52

Figure 3-1. Conversation Tasks (continued)

Task C

TRAINING:

E: *Which has more?*

E: *What about now?* and, if necessary, *Is there more water in this glass? this glass? or are they the same?*

E: *What about now?*

E: *What about now?*

Test 1:

E: *What about now?*

Test 2:

E: *Why do you think so?*

53

no response is forthcoming, "Are there more red blocks, or more yellow blocks, or are they the same?" [1]

The yellow blocks are then spread apart, and the above question or questions are repeated. Finally the child is asked, "Why do you think so?"

Conceivably, a child might respond differently to the bunching of the blocks than to the spreading of the blocks, so that the order in which these were presented might affect the results. To test this possibility thirty-two first grade children, ranging in age from six years and three months to eight years were interviewed in an independent school.[2] The method of presentation of the number task modified that used in the cross-sectional and longitudinal studies only by bunching the blocks first for half the children, randomly chosen, and spreading first for the other half. No differences were found between the protocols of children under the "bunched" or "spread" conditions.

Task B. In the second part of this experiment, only the yellow cubes are used. The child is asked to count them. Then they are spread and he is asked to indicate how many (without counting). Again they are bunched and the question "How many?" is repeated.

2. Conservation of an amount of liquid

Task C. During training the child compares the water in two identical glass tumblers, indicating when one has more water than the other, and filling them to indicate when the water is "the same."

The experimenter then empties the water from one tumbler into a shallow glass bowl, asking "What about now?" In the event of no response the question is put, "Is there more here, or more here (pointing), or are they the same?" The final question is "Why do you think so?"

3. Additional experiments

Two other experiments were included.

Stairs. This task involves the construction of steps from ten of the

---

[1] It is possible that children who really did not understand the question would "parrot" "the same." The results do not seem to indicate this but a systematic alternation of "the same," "more red," and "more yellow" would have provided better certainty.

[2] This study was planned and executed by Felice Gordis.

blocks. It was included as an easy task to provide a smooth transition from the second conservation of number tasks to the experiment with floating objects. Although this task includes some of the elements of Piaget's (1952a) seriation task involving the construction of a staircase from cards, it is much less complex. It more nearly resembles the step-building task included by Gesell and his collaborators (Thompson, 1940) in their scale of adaptive behavior. However, in the latter scale the child was not permitted to observe the experimenter's construction of the steps nor to have them in view while he attempted to reproduce them as in the present study. With the latter restriction Gesell found that only 5 per cent of the five-year-olds and 39 per cent of the six-year-olds succeeded in reproducing the model from memory.

In the present study, the experimenter, after the child has completed his responses to the questions in conservation task B, and while the child still has the eleven yellow blocks in front of him, indicates that he is going to make something with the red blocks. He puts four blocks in a row, with three, two, and one successively on top, commenting that they are "stairs." The eleventh red block is, of course, not used. He then asks the child to make stairs "like that" with his yellow blocks.

Floating and sinking objects. This experiment and the rationale for its development and inclusion are described in detail in chapter 6. Briefly, it begins with a practice session in which the child indicates what happens when a rock and a small toy boat are placed in a large pan of water. Then he is asked to indicate which of the following objects will float (stay up), and which sink (go to the bottom): two pieces of wood, two nails, two toothpicks, two stones. He is also asked to explain why he thinks they will do this. He is similarly questioned about a ball of paraffin, a ball of plasticene of the same size, and a bit of plasticene removed from it.

Order of presentation

The order of presentation of the experiments in the interview was not varied. It began with the conservation of number, tasks A and B, and continued with the construction of the stairs, and the floating and sinking of objects. It ended with the conservation of an amount of liquid, task C.

Practical considerations had led to the decision to place the experiments involving water toward the end, providing for "mop-up" following rather than during the interview.

Effects of order of presentation. So far as the conservation of number experiments were concerned, task B, conservation after counting, was deliberately placed after task A, on the assumption that the child who can maintain a demonstrated equality between two sets of objects after their transformation without resorting to counting is more facile in his thought than is the child who must rely on the prop provided by counting. Piaget theory and the eventual results of our study supported this notion. However, the question of the possible effects of the order of presentation could not really be settled until different orders had been tried. Accordingly, in the fall of 1964 a study dealing with the effects of order of the presentation of tasks was undertaken.

All of the children in attendance in the first grades in three schools in Englewood, New Jersey, were interviewed. The age range of the children was from 71 to 84 months. The socioeconomic backgrounds of the children were mixed so that the spread of abilities was not dissimilar to that in the cross-sectional and longitudinal studies. An equal number of children in each classroom were assigned at random to one of the six possible orders for presentation of the three conservation tasks, A, B, C. Interviewers were also assigned at random. A total of 164 children were interviewed and their performances in each of the three tasks scored as either conserving or not conserving. A chi-square test indicated that the slight differences in the numbers of children conserving in the various orders of presentation were not statistically significant.

Reliability

Young children are notoriously erratic in their responses in almost any sort of testing situation. This fact could impose serious limitations in interpreting the data gained from the interviews, particularly since the questions tapped a relatively small sample of each child's behavior. Further complexities arise from the difficulty of determining whether a change in response from one interview to another represents random behavior in one or both situations, learning attributable to practice, a consequence of maturation, or some combination of these factors.

The pilot study from which some of the items in the interview had been developed suggested that at least over a two-week period the children's responses were relatively stable. This finding was verified for all the conservation items in the interview schedule in the spring of 1964, when the children in a first grade in the Manhasset, New York, schools were interviewed twice with a two-week period intervening. McNemar's chi-square test showed no significant differences between the children's performances at the two testings.

Administration of the Interviews and Supplementary Tests

The children were interviewed outside their classes individually. The junior author trained ten graduate students, majors in either psychology or early childhood education, to interview and to record. They worked in teams of two, alternately conducting the interview and observing and recording the child's behavior and responses. Each interviewer, serving as recorder, observed two interviews jointly with the junior author. Their agreement with him in recording the child's responses ranged about 95 per cent for all but one of the interviewers. In the latter case the per cent of agreement fell to 84 per cent.

In the longitudinal study, one of the original interviewers continued throughout and trained two new interviewers. In the longitudinal study each interviewer did her own recording.

In the cross-sectional study the Arthur Stencil Design Test was administered at the beginning of the interview, and the Ammons Full-Range Picture Vocabulary Test at the end. Interviews and tests usually lasted from thirty-five to forty-five minutes. In a few instances the time was broken into two sessions.

The sessions in the longitudinal study, except for the final interview where three tests from the Wechsler Intelligence Scale for Children were included, were considerably shorter.

Measures of intellectual ability and academic progress

At the time the study was planned there was little evidence in the literature indicating the possible relationships between conservation abilities and intellectual abilities measured in more traditional fashion. Even less was known regarding the relation between conservation abilities and academic achievement.

School-administered tests

The results from five school-administered tests were available. One of these dealt with mental ability, the other four with progress in reading and arithmetic.

The Pintner-Cunningham Primary Test. This test was administered to the children in the first grade. The test, which is designed for kindergarten, first, and early second grade, measures seven skills: common observation (identifying objects commonly found in the usual environment); perception of esthetic differences; identification of associated objects (knowledge of relationship between objects such as key and lock); discrimination of size; perception of the elements that constitute a whole picture; picture completion; copying designs. The test manual reports reliability coefficients beween two forms ranging between .83 and .89, and correlations with the Stanford-Binet from .73 to .88.

Although it is hazardous to infer too much from the appearance of a test, a majority of items seem directly dependent on the child's ability to match elements in a concrete fashion, rather than on an ability to abstract and hold on to such elements mentally. This impression is in accord with Worcester's (1949) comment that "the test requires detailed instruction and accurate timing," and this "may account for the fact that children secure higher scores on this than on the other tests."

The four school-administered tests of academic progress are all tests developed and standardized by the Bureau of Educational Research of the Board of Education of the City of New York.

New York Test of Reading Readiness. This test was designed to provide objective evidence regarding the child's readiness to profit from instruction in reading. It has two parts, one relating to the child's understanding of stories read aloud, and the other to his ability to see likenesses and differences among printed word forms. The test manual reports reliability coefficients of .91 based on the Kuder-Richardson formula. This test was administered in the first grade. Since only the percentiles were recorded on the permanent records and the school did not keep all of the examination booklets, for the purpose of data analysis these percentiles had to be converted into the median raw score corresponding to the percentile.

New York Tests of Growth in Reading. These are a series of tests designed to measure reading achievement at different stages of reading growth. Thus Test A is a "simple survey of some beginning reading skills—the recognition of words and pictures, of phrases and pictures and sentence reading in context." Test B, for children for whom Test A is too easy, is "designed to measure achievement in reading when the child can read simple material with understanding." The manual states that Test B is likely to be appropriate at the end of the second year of reading instruction and the beginning of the third. This was the test administered to most of the children in this study in the second grade and used as the measure of reading achievement. Some youngsters, however, in the school in the lower class neighborhood, were tested on Test A and some in the middle class neighborhood on Test C.

The test manual reports reliability indices based on the Kuder-Richardson formula of .95 and .97 for the test when used in second grades.

Test B consisted of three parts dealing with sentence meaning, vocabulary, and paragraph meaning. The permanent records showed the child's grade equivalent and these were used for purposes of the present study.

New York Inventory of Mathematical Concepts. This test given in the fall of second grade has two sections dealing with premeasurement and numerical concepts. The section on premeasurement concepts requires the child to mark out pictured objects or situations in ways that will reveal his ideas of comparable shape, relative size, weight and time, gross quantity, and spatial position. The numerical concepts, also based on picture marking, include the use of symbols to express one–one correspondence, cardinal numbers to express total groupings, the use of quantitative terms, ordinal numbers, simple addition, subtraction, multiplication, division, and fractional parts.

Reliabilities based on the Kuder-Richardson formula for the two sections of the Inventory are reported to be .75 and .88.

Percentile ratings for each child's performance in the two sections of this test were posted in the school's permanent records. For purposes of this study these were converted to median raw score values.

Individually administered tests. Several considerations guided the selection of the tests that were individually administered by the staff of the present study. Some of these were practical. The tests could not take too long. They must add interest and variety to the interview.

Since one school had many children with language handicaps, they should not place too great a premium on verbal expression. Additionally, a measure that might tap abilities similar to those revealed in conservation problems, and that would provide challenge to the most able second graders was sought. The tests finally chosen had not been so extensively used as others that were considered, but they appeared to fit our criteria fairly well.

The Arthur Stencil Design Test I. In this test the child is given the task of "copying" a design, using stencils of varying color and form, placed one over another. It has been described (Arthur, 1944) as a "non-verbal test of logical thinking" and seems to demand that the child isolate and mentally manipulate the attributes of color, form, and depth. At the present time, we would infer that it draws on abilities similar to those described by Inhelder and Piaget (1964) in *The Early Growth of Logic in the Child,* a volume with which we were not familiar at the time the test was selected. On the other hand, inferences of this sort must be tentative. The number of young children in the original standardization was small (Balinsky, 1953). Arthur herself comments that "some subjects worked intuitively, selecting cards as if no other choice were possible" (p. 33). Most, however, verbalized as they worked, their words suggesting that many errors resulted from inaccurate description. She further notes that, in relation to older subjects, "Pupils scoring high tended to enjoy advanced mathematics, advanced Latin, advanced music, advanced art, mechanical and architectural drafting, and mechanics, but were less likely to enjoy subjects involving verbal facility rather than problem solving" (p. 34).

The Ammons Full-Range Picture Vocabulary Test. This test was selected as especially appropriate for use in the school in the lower class neighborhood since it has been widely used with varied populations. The test consists of sixteen cards on each of which there appear four cartoon-like line drawings. The subject chooses, by pointing, the drawing that best represents a particular word. Reliability ranges from .86 to .99 (.93 for a group of preschool children).

Correlations with the Binet vocabulary test ranging from .67 to .96 have been reported for various groups of school children, including different ethnic groups. Correlations with the full Binet at the preschool level are reported as .85 and .83.

Performance tests from the Wechsler Intelligence Scale for Children.
Three performance tests from the WISC, the Picture Arrangement,
Block Design, and Object Assembly Tests, were administered to the
children in the longitudinal study at the final interview.

The Subjects

The children were drawn from two New York City elementary
schools. One, designated here as M.C. school, is located in Brooklyn
in an area of single or double occupancy homes. Its population is predominantly middle class. The staff were already involved in several
other research projects and were extremely helpful in this one.

The second school, identified as L.C. school, is located in Manhattan's Lower East Side and serves a low-income housing project. Its
population is reported to be roughly 70 per cent Puerto Rican, 20 per
cent Negro and 10 per cent "other." L.C. school was chosen after many
unsuccessful efforts to locate a school in a lower class neighborhood
where a second language would not be a complicating factor. Many
schools were already beset by researchers or had no available space
for interviewing. L.C. school was crowded, but it had not been much
involved in research, and its principal and staff were enthusiastic about
participating in a project. They cooperated in every possible way.

In M.C. school approximately equal numbers of children were
selected at random from each class in the kindergarten, first, and
second grades. In L.C. school the class lists were divided into "Puerto
Rican" and "non-Puerto Rican" on the basis of the children's names,
and random selection was then made within these groups. In the
kindergarten, to insure that a sufficient number of non-Puerto Rican
children would remain in the longitudinal study, all the non-Puerto
Ricans were included, and only the Puerto Ricans were randomly
selected. Table 3-1 indicates the number of children in the sample
whose parents, according to the school records (consulted sometime
after the sample selection), speak English at home. In the analysis of
the data, this information has been pooled with the teacher's appraisal of the child's language in the classroom and the interviewer's
appraisal of his performance in the interview. Results are reported only
for children whose language was judged adequate on this basis.

Table 3-1. Grades, Sex, Chronological Age, IQ, and,
for School in Lower Class Area, Language
Spoken in Home of Subjects

	NUMBER IN SAMPLE		CHRONOLOGICAL AGE		PINTNER- CUNNINGHAM IQ'S		LANGUAGE	
GRADE	Boys	Girls	M	SD	M	SD	English	Other
M.C. School								
Kindergarten	25	27	66.13	4.23				
First	25	25	77.10	3.54	118.12	17.65		
Second	25	25	88.00	3.72	113.65	15.17		
L.C. School								
Kindergarten	40	40	67.09	3.14			26	54
First	25	25	77.68	4.82	104.92	18.43	29	21
Second	24	26	88.86	4.30	99.74	19.29	26	24

Categorization of the Data on Conservation

Each interview provided each child with seven opportunities to indicate whether or not he was conserving. For task A, involving the conservation of the equality of number of two rows of blocks through two transformations, the child was asked after each transformation, "What about now?" (and where this failed to elicit a response, the further question, "Are there more red or more yellow or are they the same?"). Then he was asked for an explanation, "Why do you think so?" Thus task A offered three opportunities for conservation.

Task B involved the counting of one set of the blocks used in the previous task, followed by two transformations. After each transformation the child was asked, "How many?" and accordingly had two opportunities to conserve.

Task C involved the conservation of an amount of liquid when it was poured from a tall tumbler into a shallow bowl. Here the child was asked, "What about now?" (and in the case where no response was forthcoming, "Is there more here, more here, or is it still the same?"). He was also asked for an explanation, "Why do you think so?" Thus this task afforded the child two more opportunities to indicate that he was conserving.

The child's response to each question was recorded and decisions as to whether or not it represented conservation were made independently of the rest of the interview protocol.

The fact that the tasks (with the exception of that involving conservation after counting) included enough preliminary training, so that the child presumably understood the questions and had paid attention to the transformations of the materials, eliminated many of the (to the adult) incomprehensible responses that had appeared in some of our earlier interviews. On the other hand, the standardization of the questions, and the associated lack of provision for probing suspect answers as is done in the traditional Piaget interview, meant that the responses had to be taken at face value.

Initial attempts to score the child's responses to each one of the seven questions having to do with conservation as either correct or incorrect failed to do justice to the intricacies of the children's thinking, and to the obvious relationships among the two or three responses associated with each different task. Had the study involved a wider range of ages, or had a larger variety of tasks been presented, such a simple scoring procedure might have been more feasible.

The categorization scheme that eventually evolved represented a collaboration between several individuals deeply immersed in Piaget theory and several of the interviewers who were able to infuse the recorded responses with their impressions of the children's behavior during the interviews. The scheme attempted not only to discriminate conserving from nonconserving responses, but also to identify those nonconserving responses that provided good evidence that the child's thinking was dominated by his immediate perception, as contrasted with other more ambiguous responses. It also attempted to differentiate among conserving responses those which were completely spontaneous from those in which the child might or might not be responding to clues provided by the questions put to him when he failed to answer an initial "What about now?" question.

Each of the three conservation tasks was categorized independently but the procedure for each was basically similar. It consisted of weighing the evidence for or against conservation in the child's response to each opportunity presented in a particular task. This evidence was accordingly classified in one of four categories: clearly indicative of conservation; uncertain, that is apparently indicating conservation but based on responses that could be inspired by clues in the questioning; clearly indicative of nonconservation; evidence lacking. *After* the evidence for each of the opportunities to conserve had been so classified, the evidence for the total task was weighed and the total performance on that task classified in one of five categories: clear evidence of conservation; probable evidence of conservation; uncertain evidence of conservation (a category to include the performance of a child for whom there is evidence of both conserving and not conserving, a child whose performance on this task might go either way if more evidence were available); clear evidence of nonconservation; insufficient evidence regarding conservation (a category for the child who says he does not know, gives no response, or use gestures).

Reliability of categories. All of the protocols from the cross-sectional study were categorized by the same person. For a sample of thirty protocols she and the senior investigator agreed on 90 per cent of the conservation categories. Agreement between coders for samples of the protocols taken from the longitudinal data ranged between 90 per cent and 94 per cent.

CHAPTER 4

The cross-sectional study

THE CROSS-SECTIONAL study was concerned with the extent of the understanding of the principle of conservation among young children in metropolitan elementary schools located in different socioeconomic areas and with the relationships between such understanding and age and other measures of intellectual functioning, readiness, and achievement.

The measure of the understanding of conservation was based on the children's responses to the three conservation tasks described in the previous chapter.

In considering the results, the characteristics of the two groups of children need to be kept in mind. The designations M. C. (middle class) for the Brooklyn school, and L. C. (lower class) for the Manhattan school, indicate that the neighborhoods surrounding the two schools differed markedly. Other research staffs have made similar appraisals of their status. The fact that L. C. school serves a low-cost housing project provides some clues to the economic level of the families there, as does the character of the single and double occupancy dwellings surrounding M. C. school. However, since information regarding the occupations and the aspirations of the parents of the children is lacking, the inferences that can be drawn regarding their socioeconomic status are limited.

So far as the interviewers were concerned the outstanding difference between the two schools lay in the greater ease of communication with the children in M. C. school. In general, the interviews at L. C. school necessitated spending considerably more time to establsh rapport. Even when this was satisfactorily accomplished many children seemed not to fully understand the tasks confronting them. Since over half of them came from homes in which English was a second language, such difficulties were not surprising.[1]

To insure that the children included in the study had sufficient ability in English to communicate effectively in the interview, 83 children were eliminated from the cross-sectional study. The remaining group included those for whom English was the native language plus those for whom English was a second language but who were appraised as adequate in English on two criteria. The first criterion was the interviewer's notation at the time of the interview that the child had "no difficulty with language." The second was based on a rating of the child's language made by the teacher, on a six point scale in use throughout the New York City schools. Only children whose ratings indicated an understanding of English adequate for ordinary conversation were included. Table 4-1 shows the sample of children from L. C.

Table 4-1. Grades, Sex, Chronological Age of Children
with Adequate Language from L.C. School

| | NUMBER IN SAMPLE | | CHRONOLOGICAL AGE | |
GRADE	Boys	Girls	M	SD
Kindergarten	14	17	66.96	3.10
First	16	15	77.68	4.65
Second	17	14	88.61	4.19

school remaining in the study after the children with inadequate language had been eliminated.

The data from M. C. school, where there were no problems of communication, and where the sample is larger, are obviously more dependable than those from L. C. Accordingly, throughout the study the data from M. C. school are used as the primary source of information. The L. C. data are examined for comparisons and contrasts.

[1] In a few instances, where the children did not respond to the questions in English, interviewers who spoke Spanish attempted to carry on the interview in that language, with an almost complete lack of success. The teachers, and some of our Puerto Rican colleagues, suggested that the children have such a strong set toward hearing English in school that they cannot be expected to make such a shift very readily.

Preliminary Analysis of the Data

The children's performances in each of the three tasks (A, conservation of the equality of two rows of blocks through two transformations; B, conservation of the number of a row of blocks, that have been counted, through two transformations; C, conservation of the equality of two amounts of water through one transformation) were categorized on the basis of the clarity of the evidence for conservation or non-conservation, as described in Chapter 3. A series of contingency tables were prepared. These showed, for each of the tasks, the number of children's responses falling in each category together with their corresponding responses in each of the other tasks. Separate tables showed the responses for each school, and for each grade within each school.

Difficulty of the tasks. Inspection of the contingency tables revealed some clear trends so far as the difficulty of the tasks was concerned and also suggested that some of the categories of evidence for conservation could be combined. Except in the case of the responses to task A, the first task confronting the children, the category of "probable" evidence appeared considerably less often than that of "clear" evidence. The categories of "uncertain" or "insufficient evidence" were even less frequent. They tended to be associated most often with the responses of the younger children and the children from L. C. school. In view of these findings, for most of the analyses of the data, the category of "probable" evidence was combined with that of "clear" evidence and the performances of children whose responses had been so categorized were scored 1 for conservation. Similarly the categories of "uncertain" and "insufficient" were combined with the category of "clear evidence of nonconservation" and the performances of the children in all three categories were scored 0 for conservation.

Table 4-2 shows the performance in the three tasks for the children in M. C. school. So far as the difficulty of the tasks was concerned, task B, in which 129 of the 152 children in M. C. school conserved, was clearly easier than task A in which 77 conserved, and task A easier than task C in which only 55 children conserved.

Relationships among the tasks. The extent to which children who were able to conserve in one of the tasks could also conserve in another is shown in Table 4–2.

According to the theory of Piaget, attainment of conservation in one area, such as that represented in the two tasks dealing with the blocks,

Table 4-2. Conservation Abilities of Kindergarten, First-, and Second- Grade
Children in M. C. School as Revealed in Three Different Tasks[a]

PERFORMANCE ON TASK	CONSERVING ON TASK B	NOT CONSERVING ON TASK B	TOTAL
Conserving on task A	73[b]	4	77
Not Conserving on task A	56	19	75
Total	129	23	152
	CONSERVING ON TASK C	NOT CONSERVING ON TASK C	TOTAL
Conserving on task B	52	77	129
Not Conserving on task B	3	20	23
Total	55	97	152
	CONSERVING ON TASK C	NOT CONSERVING ON TASK C	TOTAL
Conserving on task A	40	37	77
Not Conserving on task A	15	60	75
Total	55	97	152

[a] Task A: Conservation of the equality of two rows of blocks through two transformations.

B: Conservation of the number of a row of blocks that have been counted, through two transformations.

C: Conservation of the equality of two amounts of water through one transformation.

[b] This means that 73 of 77 children who conserved on task A also conserved on task B.

is associated with its attainment in other areas, such as those represented in the task dealing with an amount of liquid, but there is not an immediate shift of conservation from one area to another. One hundred and twenty-nine of the total 152 children conserved in task B, a task that required them to count the blocks before the configuration was transformed. But of these 129 children, only 73 had also been able to conserve in task A, a task involving the conservation of the equality of number of two rows of blocks through two transformations. The four children who did not conserve in task B when they had been able to conserve in task A are perhaps representative of those youngsters who become uncertain when they are questioned several times about what they presumably regard as the same task.

The third part of Table 4-2 indicates that only 40 of the 77 children who were able to conserve in task A also conserved in task C. However

15 children who conserved the amount of liquid in task C had not conserved number in task A. Presumably in the first task they had either failed to express a latent understanding, or they learned what the experimenter wanted as the interview proceeded.

Conservation patterns. When the fact of an increase in difficulty from task B to task A to task C had been established, each child's performance in the three tasks could be categorized in one of four patterns: no conservation; conservation only after counting (task B only); conservation after counting *and* conservation of the equality of two rows of blocks (task B and task A only); conservation after counting, and conservation of the equality of two rows of blocks, together with conservation of the equality of two amounts of liquid (task B, task A, task C).

Placing the children's performances in these patterns involved making changes from the original categorization in 19 cases in M. C. school. (In the case of L. C. school where the total number of children scoring 1 on any of the tasks was considerably smaller, only nine such changes were made).

The alterations were effected by rereading each protocol in its entirety. The original categorization had been based on separate considerations of each task. The general rules for making the alterations took into account the consistency of the child's responses in the three tasks, the nature of the evidence on which the scores of 0 or 1 had been based, and the child's age. Once these rules were determined, two readers independently rescored the protocols, and were in agreement on all but two cases in which joint decisions were then made.

Major Results

The major findings in the study are based on the conservation patterns described above. The trends for the two schools are compared and the performance of the children in the various patterns is related to other measures.

The extent of understanding of conservation

Table 4-3 shows the extent to which the children in both schools conserved. For both schools the percentage of children who are unable to conserve in any of the three tasks decreases from kindergarten to

Table 4-3. Number and Percent of Children Revealing Conservation
in Three Tasks[a]

TASKS IN WHICH CHILDREN CONSERVED	KINDER-GARTEN		FIRST GRADE		SECOND GRADE		TOTAL	
	N	%	N	%	N	%	N	%
M. C. School								
None	16	31	4	8	1	2	21	14
Only B	21	40	18	36	11	22	50	33
Both B & A	10	19	12	24	14	28	36	23
B, A, & C	5	9	16	32	24	48	45	29
Total	52	99	50	100	50	100	152	99
L. C. School (Children with adequate language)								
None	17	55	5	16	6	18	28	29
Only B	12	39	14	46	14	47	40	44
Both B & A	1	3	10	32	4	12	15	16
B, A, & C	1	3	2	6	7	23	10	10
Total	31	100	31	100	31	100	93	99

[a] Task A: Conservation of the equality of two sets of blocks through two transformations.

B: Conservation of the number of a set of blocks that have been counted, through two transformations.

C: Conservation of the equality of two amounts of water through one transformation.

second grade, while the number who are able to conserve in all three tasks increases. This conforms to what one would expect on the basis of Piaget theory.

Of particular interest is the fact that in M. C. school only 48 per cent of the second graders (with a mean chronological age of seven years and four months) are able to conserve in all three tasks.

The trends for the children in L. C. school are similar to those for the children in M. C. school but their progress is obviously slower, for only 23 per cent of the second graders are able to conserve in all three tasks. The performance of the first grade does not differ much from that of the kindergarten so far as the abilities represented in the combination of all three tasks are concerned, but there is relatively more progress between first and second grade.

These findings confirm those of other studies. Conservation abilities vary with the task and with the age of the child, and there are individual differences. Further, the rate at which these abilities appear seems to differ in schools with different socioeconomic backgrounds.

Relationships with other measures

Many questions have arisen concerning what can be learned from a knowledge of a child's ability to conserve that might not already be apparent from the more usual kinds of intelligence and achievement tests. Tables 4-4 through 4-8, giving means and standard deviations on intellectual, readiness, and achievement measures for children revealing different levels of conservation ability, throw some light on the possible relationships.

Intellectual ability. Table 4-4 indicates that, in general, middle class children who are conserving in all three tasks are mentally more mature than those who are not. This table also suggests as do those following that the differences between those who can conserve after counting (that is, in task B) and those who can also conserve number without counting (task A) are, as might be expected, not very great. The trends for the lower class group are, as in most of the measures demanding verbal facility, much less clear.

Table 4-5, dealing with the children's performance in the Stencil Design test, a test described as a nonverbal test of logical thinking, shows, particularly for the middle class children, a rather consistent correspondence with conservation ability. On a total group basis similar trends are apparent in the lower class group. Table 4-6, presenting the results for the vocabulary tests, shows somewhat similar but less consistent trends.

Readiness and achievement. Tables 4-7 and 4-8 indicate the extent to which the children who perform well in the conservation tasks also do well in beginning reading and arithmetic. Such an advantage is greater in kindergarten and first grade than it is later when conservation ability becomes more widespread.

Obviously, all of the measures reported are to a considerable extent measuring similar abilities. The Ammons Full-Range Picture Vocabulary, the Pintner, the Reading Readiness tests, and the Mathematical Concepts Inventory, for example, all demand that the child find a picture to illustrate a particular word or concept. Some of the items on the Numerical Concepts test involve a recognition of one-one correspondence bordering on the ability to conserve. Tables A-1 through A-3 in

Table 4-4. Mean IQ's (Based on Pintner-Cunningham Primary Test)[a] of Children Revealing Different Conservation Abilities[b]

TASKS IN WHICH CHILDREN CONSERVED	FIRST GRADE			SECOND GRADE			TOTAL		
	N	M	SD	N	M	SD	N	M	SD
M. C. School									
None	4	107.00	17.80	0	0.	0.	4	107.00	17.80
Only A	18	115.67	19.08	9	109.78	12.17	27	113.70	17.08
Both B & A	11	116.18	16.56	13	107.92	11.89	24	111.71	14.52
B, A, & C	14	126.00	15.05	24	118.21	16.70	38	121.08	16.36
Total	47	118.13	17.66	46	113.65	15.17	93	115.94	16.54
L. C. School (Children with adequate language)									
None	2	109.50	12.02	5	106.40	8.53	7	107.29	8.65
Only A	12	112.25	17.46	13	111.46	19.37	25	111.84	18.10
Both B & A	10	101.00	17.75	4	100.00	15.03	14	100.70	16.45
B, A, & C	2	130.00	26.87	7	102.14	24.89	9	108.33	26.57
Total	26	109.08	18.66	29	106.76	18.72	55	107.85	18.55

[a] Scores on school-administered tests not available for all subjects.

[b] Task A: Conservation of the equality of two sets of blocks through two transformations.

B: Conservation of the number of a set of blocks that have been counted, through two transformations.

C: Conservation of the equality of two amounts of water through one transformation.

Table 4-5. Mean Scores on Stencil Design Test of Children Revealing Different Conservation Abilities[a]

TASKS IN WHICH CHILDREN CONSERVED	KINDERGARTEN			FIRST GRADE			SECOND GRADE			TOTAL		
	N	M	SD	N	M	SD	N	M	SD	N	M	SD
M. C. School												
None	16	2.75	2.21	4	1.75	2.36	1	3.00	0.00	21	2.57	2.16
Only B	21	3.05	2.13	18	3.33	1.78	11	5.45	2.34	50	3.68	2.23
Both B & A	10	5.00	2.94	12	4.17	2.41	14	5.21	3.04	36	4.81	2.78
B, A, & C	5	5.20	1.30	16	3.81	1.76	24	6.67	2.88	45	5.49	2.71
Total	52	3.54	2.42	50	3.56	2.02	50	5.92	2.85	152	4.33	2.68
L. C. School (Children with adequate language)												
None	17	0.71	0.92	5	1.80	1.92	6	5.17	4.40	28	1.86	2.81
Only B	12	1.75	1.82	14	3.71	2.37	14	3.57	3.18	40	3.07	2.63
Both B & A	1	3.00	0.00	10	3.30	1.25	4	4.50	1.29	15	3.60	1.30
B, A, & C	1	1.00	0.00	2	7.50	4.95	7	4.86	4.30	10	5.00	4.27
Total	31	1.19	1.42	31	3.52	2.41	31	4.29	3.46	93	3.00	2.86

[a] Task A: Conservation of the equality of two sets of blocks through two transformations.
   B: Conservation of the number of a set of blocks that have been counted, through two transformations.
   C: Conservation of the equality of two amounts of water through one transformation.

Table 4-6. Mean Scores on Ammons Picture Vocabulary Test of Children Revealing Different Conservation Abilities[a]

TASKS IN WHICH CHILDREN CONSERVED	KINDERGARTEN			FIRST GRADE			SECOND GRADE			TOTAL		
	N	M	SD	N	M	SD	N	M	SD	N	M	SD
M. C. School												
None	16	22.44	4.24	4	28.50	2.65	1	24.00	0.00	21	23.67	4.52
Only B	21	25.76	4.89	18	26.22	4.18	11	28.64	4.25	50	26.56	4.56
Both B & A	10	25.50	4.22	12	27.92	5.40	14	27.79	6.08	36	27.19	5.35
B, A, & C	5	29.60	3.36	16	29.44	5.54	24	31.58	6.17	45	30.60	5.70
Total	52	25.06	4.81	50	27.84	4.93	50	29.72	5.92	152	27.51	5.92
L. C. School (Children with adequate language)												
None	17	17.18	4.29	5	19.20	5.40	6	26.17	7.70	28	19.46	6.29
Only B	12	15.17	4.43	14	21.71	3.93	14	23.79	7.35	40	20.47	6.47
Both B & A	1	25.00	0.00	10	20.70	4.85	4	22.25	5.74	15	21.40	4.87
B, A, & C	1	22.00	0.00	2	19.00	5.66	7	22.29	7.04	10	21.60	6.20
Total	31	16.81	4.61	31	20.81	4.45	31	23.71	6.96	93	20.44	6.11

[a] Task A: Conservation of the equality of two sets of blocks through two transformations.
    B: Conservation of the number of a set of blocks that have been counted, through two transformations.
    C: Conservation of the equality of two amounts of water through one transformation.

Table 4-7. Mean Reading Performance of Children Revealing
Different Conservation Abilities[a]

TASKS IN WHICH CHILDREN CONSERVED	N. Y. Test of Reading Readiness[b] FIRST GRADE[c]			N. Y. Test of Growth in Reading[b] SECOND GRADE[d]		
	N	M	SD	N	M	SD
M.C. School						
None	4	33.13	13.68	1	2.90	0.00
Only B	17	43.35	5.36	9	3.24	0.70
Both B & A	12	44.08	4.57	14	3.29	0.81
B, A, & C	15	46.73	3.23	20	3.73	0.98
Total	48	43.74	6.50	44	3.47	0.88
L.C. School (Children with adequate language)						
None	4	29.38	15.20	5	2.50	0.38
Only B	13	42.65	3.97	13	3.20	1.41
Both B & A	10	37.75	5.19	4	2.95	0.39
B, A, & C	2	41.50	2.83	7	2.49	0.49
Total	29	39.05	7.80	29	2.87	1.03

[a] Task A: Conservation of the equality of two sets of blocks through two transformations.
B: Conservation of the number of a set of blocks that have been counted, through two transformations.
C: Conservation of the equality of two amounts of water through one transformation.
[b] Scores on school-administered test not available for all subjects.
[c] Based on estimated raw scores converted from percentile ranks.
[d] Based on estimated grade norms.

the Appendix present the intercorrelations for the variables other than conservation ability.

Prediction of conservation ability from other measures. Two of the measures of intellectual functioning, the Ammons Picture Vocabulary test, and the Arthur Stencil Design Test, were individually administered to every child in the study. Assuming that the first test provides a valid appraisal of language development, and the second of the development of logical thinking, the question of the relative contribution of each to the ability to conserve can be investigated. Piaget's position is that the child's language reflects his logic, and that the mere acquisition of vocabulary will have little effect on his thinking.

A discriminant function analysis was done to reveal the predictive contribution that each of the three variables of chronological age, lan-

Table 4-8. Mean Mathematical Performance[a] of Second-Grade Children
Revealing Different Conservation Abilities[b]

TASKS IN WHICH CHILDREN CONSERVED	PREMEASUREMENT CONCEPTS[c]			NUMERICAL CONCEPTS[c]		
	N	M	SD	N	M	SD
M.C. School						
None	1	30.50	0.00	1	35.50	0.00
Only B	9	34.39	2.45	9	29.00	4.85
Both B & A	14	34.82	2.35	14	28.43	4.23
B, A, & C	24	36.79	1.84	24	33.17	2.87
Total	48	35.64	2.44	48	31.05	4.31
L.C. School (Children with adequate language)						
None	6	34.08	1.91	6	25.67	4.39
Only B	13	30.65	6.68	13	28.88	3.86
Both B & A	4	32.38	1.49	4	25.63	5.25
B, A, & C	7	33.86	3.17	7	26.57	9.40
Total	30	32.32	4.89	30	27.27	5.73

[a] Scores on school-administered tests not available for all subjects.
[b] Task A: Conservation of the equality of two sets of blocks through two trans-
    formations.
   B: Conservation of the number of a set of blocks that have been counted,
      through two transformations.
   C: Conservation of the equality of two amounts of water through one trans-
      formation.
[c] Based on estimated raw scores converted from percentile ranks on N. Y. Inventory
   of Mathematical Concepts.

guage ability as measured by the Ammons, and logical ability as measured by the Stencil Design test makes to the ability to conserve.

For this analysis, the children who were only able to conserve in
task B (conservation after counting) were combined with those who
were able to conserve in both task A (conservation without counting)
and task B since the earlier analyses had indicated that these two
groups did not differ greatly on other measures. Accordingly, for each
of the two schools, the differences between means relative to variabil-
ity and correlation in chronological age, vocabulary, and stencil scores
were considered for three groups of children, those who did not conserve at all, those conserving in task B only or in both task A and task
B, and those who conserved in all three tasks. Table 4-9 shows the F
ratios for each of the three variables.

Table 4-9. *F* Ratios for Three Variables

	F RATIO	
VARIABLE	M. C. School	L. C. School
CA	18.22	11.57
Vocabulary Score	15.03	0.59
Stencil Score	9.97	5.28

In both schools the variable that best predicts ability to conserve is clearly chronological age. In M. C. school, vocabulary contributes more to the prediction of conservation than do those abilities represented in the Stencil Design test. On the basis of these results, one may either question the assumptions made regarding the measures used, or the validity of Piaget's position regarding the relationships of language and logic, or observe that once again, for children from middle class backgrounds, good verbal ability is associated with progress in other areas.

The picture for L. C. school, where verbal facility is relatively rare, is somewhat different. Since fewer children are involved and the range of scores in all the measures is narrow, speculation must be cautious. But clearly some children, while relatively low in language ability, have some kinds of elementary logical abilities that show up in both the conservation tasks and the Stencil test. To this extent, Piaget's contention is supported.

Subsidiary Findings

The data of the study have yielded some information related to questions that were not so much in the foreground of concern when the study was planned, but that have assumed increasing interest as it has progressed. One such question, as we have suggested, relates to the role that language plays in the development of the logical abilities involved in conservation. The descriptions and explanations the children gave have been examined with this question in view. Because of the nature of the data, the conclusions are necessarily tentative.

Descriptions and explanations used by the children

The analysis of the children's conservation abilities to this point has been concerned with the correctness of their understanding or judgments. One can also examine their responses in terms of how they describe the transformations they have seen regardless of the logic they reveal.

Descriptions of the transformations. In tasks A and C, after the child had completed the initial training designed to focus his attention on the appropriate use of the terms "more" and "same," the interviewer rearranged the blocks in task A, and in task C, poured the water from the glass into the bowl. The question then posed to the child was, "What about now?" and to those who failed to respond, "Is there more here, more here, or are they the same?"

The children whose replies indicated that the equality of number or amount changed when the configurations changed tended to agree that there were "more yellow blocks" when the red blocks were bunched. When the yellow blocks were spread, two-thirds of the children indicated that there were more yellow blocks. When the water was poured from the glass into the dish, 87 per cent indicated that there was more water in the glass.

Some researchers (for example, Zimles, 1963) have argued that the child's response to these situations may be determined primarily by what the adult manipulates. If this were the case one might expect the child to perceive the red blocks as "more" after their bunching. On the other hand, in task C the interviewer does manipulate the glass in pouring, and not the bowl.

The effect of the experimenter's actions on the child's responses probably deserves further study. For example, one of our researchers (Felice Gordis) working with first graders found that children who had conserved an amount of liquid through one transformation were less likely to change to nonconservation in a second transformation if they poured the liquid themselves.

Explanations of the transformations. Just as a child's description of the situation after a transformation has occurred may reveal that his attention is focused on something other than what the adult intends, so his explanation may throw light on his thinking. Especially in the cases where he is not conserving, the child's explanations may indicate the nature of his confusions and provide the adult with clues to the kinds of experience that may help to eradicate them.

From the initiation of the study we were interested in an analysis of the explanations that would go beyond scoring them as conserving or not conserving. Various kinds of analyses were attempted. Some involved rather large leaps of adult inference from the children's relatively short, although frequently complex, statements. Others stuck closely to the words the children used, counting adjectives, verbs, and so on. None of the analyses were completely satisfactory. More times than we care to remember, some conceptual framework, developed on the basis of one sample of children's responses, had to be abandoned because it would not fit a second sample, or even the first sample when used at a later date or by a different researcher. These difficulties very likely reflect both the nature of the children's thinking and its expression in language. It is hard to impose a system on their explanations simply because they themselves have not yet acquired a really systematic way of viewing the world.

The nature of the data must also be considered. For each task, the children had only one opportunity for explanation. Furthermore, the interviewers accepted all explanations at face value and did not probe further, as they would have in an interview in the classic Piaget style. Thus the responses may not represent the child's "best" or most profound thinking. On the other hand, they are relatively uncontaminated by the influence of the adult interrogator.

Although it would seem reasonable to find explanations among children who are conserving differing from those offered by children who are not conserving, study indicated that a majority of both groups' explanations fell into similar categories. Three large categories emerged for each task.

For task A, the most frequent explanation involved references to either the action of the interviewer or to the movement of the blocks, as for example, "moved," "spread," "pushed," or, "taken (or not taken) away." Other popular explanations, used about equally, involved the description of one or both sets of blocks, as for example, "a pile," or "a line."

For task C, the preponderant explanation involved the description of one vessel, as, "big," "tall," "low," "short," "skinny," "wide," "thin," "flat." Other explanations used similar words but described both vessels. A third type of explanation focused on the level of the water, as "lower," "higher," "up to here."

Some children did not volunteer explanations or gave responses that could not be categorized in this fashion, but approximately two-thirds of the explanations given did fall into one of these three categories. Such explanations could then be examined in relation to the child's assertion, or failure to assert, that the number of blocks or the amount of water remained the same.

So far as task A is concerned, in M. C. school the children who indicate that the number of blocks is the same, most frequently give an explanation involving "movement," implying either that the experimenter only (or in the children's language "just") moved the object about, or more specifically did not take any away. But children who do not assert that the number remains the same also use this explanation, and in about the same frequency as they describe one or both sets of blocks.

In task C, the children who maintain the equality of the two amounts of water are about evenly divided between those who describe one vessel and those who describe two. The older children are most likely to describe only one vessel. But a considerable number of children, regardless of whether or not they think the amount of liquid remains the same, describe both vessels. However, children who conserve seem to be more likely to give more detailed responses about both vessels than those who are not conserving. In general, the children in M. C. school who describe only one vessel use the comparative form of the adjective they choose regardless of whether they indicate that one vessel has more water than the other.

According to Piaget theory, a number of the children who indicate that the amount of water is the same could be expected to deal directly with the relationships between the dimensions of the two vessels explaining that the one that is taller and narrower is equivalent to the other that is shorter and wider. None of the children in the present study are this explicit, unless "This one is tall and skinny, this one short and fat," a response occurring once among the conservers, and once among the nonconservers, is included. On the other hand, some of the comparisons such as, "This one is high, and this one is wide," particularly when accompanied by gestures, may indicate that the child is aware of the unspecified dimension.

Bruner (1964) has suggested that the use of appropriate terminology might help the child in making appropriate comparisons. He notes that nonconservers are likely to use global words such as "big" and "little," while conservers use dimensional terms such as "wide," "narrow," "tall," "short." Children who confound global and dimensional terms are not likely to conserve.

The data of this study do not seem to indicate any very clear-cut relationship between the terms the child uses and his conviction that the amount of liquid has or has not changed. Global comparisons appear only slightly more often among children who do not specify that the amount of liquid is the same than among those who do. Confounded responses are rare, but occur among both groups.

The use of the terms "fat" and "skinny" is interesting. About a quarter of the responses include one or both of them. Some of the responses suggest that they are used as terms equivalent to "big" and "little," but in other instances they seem to serve as a childish shorthand for "short and wide," "tall and narrow."

Responses that focus on the level of the water are mostly variations of "it's up to here." Some children specify a comparison between the levels in the two vessels, but most of them pay attention to only one vessel.

One first grader, who had indicated that there was more water in the glass than in the bowl, went on to explain that she thought this was so, "Because if the water in the bowl were in the glass it would be the same amount." This response, not a typical one, illustrates how the child may recognize the initial equivalence of the amounts without firm conviction regarding the equivalence following the transformation in appearance.

The explanations offered by the children in L. C. school do not reveal any specific trends. A number of children failed to offer any explanations, but not so many were as unresponsive in this task which came toward the end of the interview as they had been in the first conservation task. The most striking feature of the explanations that were offered is their dependence on the terms "big," "little," and "small." "Fat" and "skinny," so popular among the children in M. C. school, are rarely used. Also of interest is the fact that the L. C. children almost never use comparative forms, such as "bigger" or "smaller." Confounded responses involving a mixture of global and dimensional terms are equally rare.

On the whole, this examination of the children's descriptions and explanations serves only to highlight the conclusions reached through the more rigorous weighing of evidence for and against conservation.

Most of the children do not appear to have any coherent system for handling the problem of "sameness" when it relates to quantity and number. In the middle class group most of them have the requisite vocabulary, but many do not yet apply it in ways that the adult would regard as appropriate. The lower class group is further handicapped by an apparent lack of knowledge of terms.

Sex differences

The question of the relationships between language and the development of logical thinking leads to the further question as to whether girls may possibly be advanced over boys in conservation because of their more rapid progress in language development. On the other hand, since there is also evidence that boys tend to excel in mathematics, a finding of superior conservation ability on the part of the boys would not be surprising. However, the data of the present study provide no evidence that the performance in the conservation tasks differs for the two sexes.

Performance in the stairs task

In the preliminary analysis of the data, each child's performance in the task involving the copying of a set of steps was scored according to a scheme based on the adequacy of the copy. There were no apparent relationships to the other tasks, and the task was eliminated from further analysis. A later and more intensive review of Piaget's studies of seriation and acquaintance with the results of studies where children had been given various kinds of seriation tasks suggested a reexamination of the data. Performance in the task was rescored on the basis of either copying or not copying the model correctly.

It will be recalled that the stairs task in the present study permitted the child to keep the model in view while he built his copy. Accordingly it would seem that he would not need to hold the relationships among four blocks, three blocks, two blocks and one block in mind but could merely match his construction to the model. A comparison of the results of the present study with those reported by Gesell (Thompson, 1940) for performance of the task without the model indicated that our task is, as anticipated, very much easier. Nevertheless some relationship to conservation ability is indicated in Table 4-10 in which conservation patterns 2 and 3 have been combined indicates.

Table 4-10. Number of Children in M. C. School in Three Conservation
Patterns Copying or Not Copying Model of Steps

TASKS IN WHICH CHILDREN CONSERVED	KINDERGARTEN		FIRST GRADE		SECOND GRADE	
	Copying	Not Copying	Copying	Not Copying	Copying	Not Copying
None	7	9	2	2	1	0
A, or B & A	17	14	23	7	19	6
A, B, & C	5	0	13	3	24	0
Total	29	23	38	12	44	6

The trends for L. C. school are similar except that to a greater extent those who do not copy do not conserve. This undoubtedly reflects the generally poorer responses of the children in L. C. school. It is interesting, however, that the proportion of children who conserve and do not copy is also smaller for L. C. school. One speculates that some of the more test-wise middle class children, as they appeared to do in some other situations, read into this easy task something more than was intended, and accordingly failed it. Some youngsters, for example, tried to use eleven blocks even though the model had only ten.

Summary

The results of the cross-sectional study confirmed the relevance of Piaget's theory and experimentation to the study of young children in the beginning years of school.

The children's performances in the three conservation tasks fell in patterns corresponding to the sequence in which progress toward operational thought, as described by Piaget, is presumed to be made. The extent of understanding of conservation among the middle class children is indicated by the fact that only 48 per cent of the second-grade children, in the middle class school, with a mean chronological age of seven years and four months, were able to conserve in all three of the tasks. Piaget theory typically views seven years as the pivotal age between the period of formation or elaboration of operational thought, and the period of structuration following its attainment.

Piaget's contention that maturation plays a considerable part in the development of logical abilities is supported by the close relationship between performance in the conservation tasks and chronological age. But this study also provides evidence for Piaget's further observation that maturational factors must be supported by experiential factors. The performances of the children in the lower class school show a sequential development with age similar to that of the children in the middle class school, but much slower in pace. At the second grade level only 23 per cent of the children in the lower class school conserve in all three tasks.

When the children's performances in the conservation tasks are examined in relation to their performances in other tests of mental ability and academic achievement, it is apparent that the understanding of conservation does tend to go with these other measures. In general, children who are able to conserve at an early age do better in other tests related to mental ability and to beginning reading and arithmetic.

The findings of the cross-sectional study supported the importance of continued investigation of the understanding of conservation, and raised the question of whether the apparent sequence of its development and the relationships found between it and other measures could be substantiated in a study of longer duration.

CHAPTER 5

The longitudinal study

THE LONGITUDINAL study was designed to provide information on questions that have both theoretical and practical significance. Piaget's theory is clearly developmental. However, in his own experimentation he has usually tested different groups of children of varied ages with different problems. He has not been much concerned with individual variation over tasks, nor with individual differences in progress from one level of development to another. Some investigators have dealt with the individual child's consistency from one task to another, but the question of his progress in handling more complex tasks as he grows older calls for a longitudinal approach. Inhelder (Tanner & Inhelder, 1953) has commented on some European studies but we are unaware of any longitudinal studies in the United States. To verify longitudinally the sequence of development that Piaget has described on the basis of cross-sectional investigation would be to add support to his theory.

From a somewhat more practical stance, it seems likely that the finding that a particular child conserves, as in the three tasks included in the cross-sectional study, has rather limited prognostic value for his learning in the classroom unless one also knows something of his history. Thus a particular second grader may have only recently arrived at an understanding of the principle while his peer may have had a good grasp of it for a year or two. Piaget has indicated that during the period of acquisition of the concept, children vacillate in their understanding. Nevertheless one would anticipate that the child who conserved in all three tasks in kindergarten would derive somewhat different meaning from his experiences in the ensuing two years than would the child who did not succeed in the three tasks until the second grade. There is a further question as to the effects of the longitudinal investigation on the child. Perhaps the experience of having the tasks posed to him on successive occasions encourages him to think about them and brings him to an understanding of the principle involved earlier than would otherwise be the case.

These were some of the considerations underlying our plan to include the kindergarten children who had participated in the cross-sectional study in a longitudinal study. Their progress could be appraised individually. In addition, their progress as a group when they reached first and second grade could be compared with that of their counterparts who had been interviewed only once in the cross-sectional study.

The Longitudinal Population

The original kindergarten groups were described in Chapter 4. Those children who continued to attend the two schools were reinterviewed in the spring of 1962 while they were still in kindergarten, in the fall of 1962 and the spring of 1963 when they were in first grade, and in the fall of 1963 when they were in second grade. Table 5-1 describes the

Table 5-1. Sex, Chronological Age, and IQ of Children in the Longitudinal Study.

SCHOOL	NUMBER IN SAMPLE (5 successive interviews)		CHRONOLOGICAL AGE AT LAST INTERVIEW (second grade)		FINTNER-CUNNINGHAM IQ'S	
	Boys	Girls	M	SD	M	SD
M. C.	20	21	88.07	3.13	120.80	20.25
L. C.	13	11	89.74	2.84	106.52	19.50

longitudinal population, the children who remained in the study for five successive interviews.

The middle class sample dwindled from 52 to 41. In the school in the lower class neighborhood, the original kindergarten sample had included 78 children, of whom only 31 proved to have adequate language, and so could be used as subjects in the cross-sectional study. Twenty-four of these children continued throughout the longitudinal study.

All of the children originally interviewed in kindergarten in the lower class school who remained in the school were reinterviewed at six-month intervals, regardless of their language status. Some of these children became adequate in language as the study progressed, and are included in some of the analyses involving comparisons of longitudinal and cross-sectional samples, but are otherwise not used in the longitudinal study.

Interviewing Procedures

In the longitudinal study, the interviews were conducted in the same manner as in the cross-sectional study, except that the interviewing and recording were done by the same person. Four of the interviewers for the cross-sectional study continued into the spring 1962 interviewing. One of these remained with the study and served as an interviewer until its conclusion. One new interviewer was added in the fall of 1962, and a second in the spring of 1962. The latter also continued as an interviewer during the remainder of the study.

In each instance where new interviewers were added they were trained by an experienced interviewer who had been involved in the previous round of interviewing. Although no objective measure is available, it is likely that the interviewing in the longitudinal study was somewhat more skillful than in the cross-sectional. The interviewers for the longitudinal study had had more experience with the interview schedule, were more closely involved in the study, and had more opportunity to know the children.

The Stencil Design and Ammons Picture Vocabulary tests, given as part of the interviews in the cross-sectional study, were not repeated in the longitudinal. The Block Design, Picture Arrangement, and Object Assembly tests from the Wechsler Intelligence Scale for Children were administered at the final interview. Aside from this, each interview in the longitudinal study was essentially a repetition of the initial interview.

The effects of short term repetition of the interview were discussed in Chapter 3. So far as the interviewers were able to tell, the children generally reacted positively to the interviews, despite having been through them several times before. They indicated that they remembered the materials, especially those used for the "floating and sinking" portions of the interview, but they did not appear to remember the tasks.

Categorization and Scoring of the Data

In the longitudinal study the protocols related to the conservation tasks were categorized for evidence of conservation in exactly the same way as those in the cross-sectional study (see pp. 63–64). Each child's performance in each of the three tasks at each interview was then scored 1 if the performance indicated that he was conserving, 0 if evidence of conservation was lacking. These scores provided the information for categorization of the child's performance in each successive interview in one of four patterns, as in the cross-sectional study. The scores were also used in calculating the sum of standard scores which served as the measure of the child's progress in understanding conservation.

Conservation patterns. In the cross-sectional study the data indicated that the three conservation tasks differed in difficulty. The data supported the assumption that progress in acquiring the conservation abilities tested could be represented in four patterns: (1) no conservation in any task; (2) conservation in task B (conservation of number after counting); (3) conservation in both task B and task A (conservation of number); (4) conservation in tasks B, A, and C (conservation of an amount of liquid). Tasks A and B appeared to be somewhat comparable in level of difficulty while task C appeared to be considerably harder. Examination of the longitudinal data indicated that the great majority of the children's performances at any interview could also be categorized in one of these four patterns. However, just as in the cross-sectional study, the performances of a few children (12 per cent in both studies) did not conform to any one of these patterns. The most common variation was the performance of the child who appeared to be able to conserve in task C when he had not conserved in an easier task. In the longitudinal study for purposes of the conservation pattern analysis the scores of children whose performances fell into these irregular patterns were altered to conform to one of the four predominant patterns. The procedures used for making such alterations were the same as for the cross-sectional study (see p. 69).

Sum of standard scores. The scores, 1 for evidence of conservation, 0 when such evidence was lacking, were summed up for each interview. Thus at any interview a child's raw score might be 0, 1, 2, or 3. Tables A-4 and A-5 in the Appendix show the scores of each child in each successive interview, together with the means and standard deviations of the total group of children at each successive interviewing period.

The raw scores for each child in each successive interview were transformed into standard scores. Tables A-6 and A-7 in the Appendix show these standard scores and their sums for each child. The sum of standard scores provides an index to the child's conservation ability that allows most credit to the child who conserves early, and continues to conserve, as contrasted with the child who begins to conserve at a time when conservation is the predominant trend for children of his age. It serves as a measure of the individual's progress in relation to that of his group.

Results

Certain features of the design of the longitudinal study should be kept in mind in considering the results.

Repetition of the tasks. The conservation tasks were always the same. Lacking evidence on the comparative difficulty of tasks that might have been used for alternate forms of the interview, we were guided by our finding that repetition on a short term (two-week) basis did not alter performance. We can only speculate on what the results might have been had the tasks been more varied, or had there been more of them.

No tasks specifically designed to test the transfer or the generality of conservation abilities were included, although the clear vision afforded by hindsight suggests that such tasks would have been highly appropriate for the final interview.

Innovations in mathematics program. So far as we are aware, none of the children in the study received any direct instruction in conservation tasks. However, the children in M. C. school were introduced to a "new" mathematics program in the second semester of kindergarten. It involved a small amount of experimentation with Cuisenaire material. When the children were in first grade, material dealing with sets (Suppes, 1961) was used to supplement the regular arithmetic program. Work with equations and inequalities was also included. Instruction of this sort seems likely to have more influence on the ability to conserve, as measured by the tasks used in this study, than would the more traditional arithmetic emphasizing counting and computation.

With these limitations in view, several questions can be asked. When children are followed longitudinally, does the ability to conserve in different kinds of tasks follow the same sequence as appeared in the cross-sectional study? To what extent do individuals vary, both in conformity to the sequence and in progress through it? Do the conservation abilities of children tested at six-month intervals from kindergarten into second grade differ from those of children of similar age and background who have not been previously tested? How does the progress in conservation ability made by children from lower class backgrounds differ from that made by their peers from middle class backgrounds? How is progress in the ability to conserve as measured by scores in successive interviews related to other measures of intellectual ability and academic achievement?

The sequence of development of conservation

The order of difficulty of the tasks suggested by Piaget's theory and revealed in the cross-sectional study is confirmed in the longitudinal study.

Table 5-2 shows that the number of children who are unable to conserve in any task decreases steadily from interview to interview, while the number who are able to conserve in all three tasks tends to increase. The trends for children who are conserving only in task B, or in both tasks B and A but not in C, are not quite so definite, suggesting, as in the cross-sectional study, that these tasks are somewhat comparable in difficulty. Also, as in the cross-sectional study, there is somewhat less regularity and considerably less progress for the children in L. C. school than for those in M. C. school.

It is interesting to note that by the time they reach second grade and have passed their seventh birthdays, 76 per cent of the longitudinal group in the middle class school are conserving in all three tasks. This finding corresponds nicely with Piaget's statement that seven is the age at which 75 per cent of the Geneva children reveal an understanding of conservation.

Table 5-2. Number of Children Revealing Conservation in Three Tasks[a]
in Successive Interviews

TASKS IN WHICH CHILDREN CONSERVED	KINDERGARTEN		FIRST GRADE		SECOND GRADE
	Fall 1961	Spring 1962	Fall 1962	Spring 1963	Fall 1963
M. C. School (41 children)					
None	12	10	3	3	1
Only B	15	7	10	10	3
Both B & A	9	14	11	7	6
B, A, & C	5	10	17	21	31
L. C. School (24 children)					
None	14	11	7	3	1
Only B	10	9	11	11	14
Both B & A	0	2	5	4	2
B, A, & C	0	2	1	6	7

[a] Task A: Conservation of the equality of two sets of blocks through two transformations.
  B: Conservation of the number of a set of blocks that have been counted, through two transformations.
  C: Conservation of the equality of two amounts of water through one transformation.

Sequence for individual children. Table 5-2 depicts the performances of the same groups of children at successive time intervals in what may be regarded as a series of cross-sectional studies. In contrast, Tables 5-3 and 5-4 trace the progress made by the children from one interview to the next.

The top matrix shows the shifts in the performances of the children from the first to the second interview. In M. C. school, for example, twelve children are in pattern 1, not conserving in any task, in the first interview. Of these twelve, five remain in the same pattern at the next interview, five move ahead to pattern 2, conserving in the easiest task, while one moves to pattern 3 and one to pattern 4. Of the fifteen children who in the first interview are in pattern 2, five regress to no conservation in the second interview; one stays the same; seven move on to pattern 3; two are also able to handle the task involving an amount of liquid, and are categorized in pattern 4.

Table 5-3. Patterns of Conservation Abilities of 41 Children Revealed in Interviews Repeated at Six-month Intervals from Mid-kindergarten through Mid-second Grade in M. C. School

Markov Matrices

INTERVIEW 1	INTERVIEW 2				
Pattern[a]	1	2	3	4	Total
1	5	5	1	1	12
2	5	1	7	2	15
3	0	0	5	4	9
4	0	1	1	3	5

INTERVIEW 2	INTERVIEW 3				
Pattern[a]	1	2	3	4	Total
1	1	5	2	2	10
2	1	2	2	2	7
3	0	3	7	4	14
4	1	0	0	9	10

INTERVIEW 3	INTERVIEW 4				
Pattern[a]	1	2	3	4	Total
1	1	1	0	1	3
2	1	4	2	3	10
3	1	4	4	2	11
4	0	1	1	15	17

INTERVIEW 4	INTERVIEW 5				
Pattern[a]	1	2	3	4	Total
1	0	0	1	2	3
2	1	2	3	4	10
3	0	1	1	5	7
4	0	0	1	20	21

[a] Pattern 1: Conservation in no task
2: Conservation in task B only
3: Conservation in both task B and task A
4: Conservation in tasks B, A, and C

Table 5-4. Patterns of Conservation Abilities of 24 Children Revealed in
Interviews Repeated at Six-month Intervals from Mid-kindergarten
through Mid-second Grade in L. C. School
Markov Matrices

INTERVIEW 1	INTERVIEW 2				
Pattern[a]	1	2	3	4	Total
1	10	4	0	0	14
2	1	5	2	2	10
3	0	0	0	0	0
4	0	0	0	0	0

INTERVIEW 2	INTERVIEW 3				
Pattern[a]	1	2	3	4	Total
1	5	5	1	0	11
2	2	5	2	0	9
3	0	1	1	0	2
4	0	0	1	1	2

INTERVIEW 3	INTERVIEW 4				
Pattern[a]	1	2	3	4	Total
1	1	3	2	1	7
2	2	5	1	3	11
3	0	3	1	1	5
4	0	0	0	1	1

INTERVIEW 4	INTERVIEW 5				
Pattern[a]	1	2	3	4	Total
1	0	3	0	0	3
3	0	10	0	1	11
3	1	1	0	2	4
4	0	0	2	4	6

[a] Pattern 1: Conservation in no task
  2: Conservation in task B only
  3: Conservation in both task B and task A
  4: Conservation in tasks B, A, and C

Prediction of shifts from one pattern to another. Examination of the successive matrices provides some information on the probability that a child whose performance falls in a particular pattern at one interview will move to a different pattern at the next.

It is clear, as it was in the cross-sectional study, that the difference between tasks B and A is not great and the children may vacillate somewhat in their performance in these two tasks. Once they succeed in these two tasks in the earlier interviews, their performance appears to be somewhat stabilized. Note that a preponderance of children whose performance falls in pattern 3 in the first and second interviews either remain there or move ahead in the next interview (100 per cent at the second interview, 79 per cent at the third interview). By interview 4, the picture changes, with 45 per cent regressing to a less advanced pattern. This performance can, however, be viewed against the trend for the whole group, of whom 21, or half, have now reached pattern 4.

As might be anticipated, performance in pattern 4 remains relatively stable. Once that pattern is reached, when all interviews are considered, there are only five instances (9 per cent) where regression occurs at the next interview.

When all the patterns and all the interviews are considered, the children in the middle class school either move in the expected direction or stay the same 83 per cent of the time.

Table 5-4 shows the progress from interview to interview of the children in the lower class school. The trends appear similar to those in the middle class school, but the number of children moving beyond pattern 2 is too small for generalization.

Individual variation in progress

The extent of individual variations in progress toward conservation should be apparent from the preceding discussion and from reference to the individual scores for each testing to be found in Tables A-4 and A-5 in the Appendix.

We anticipated that, despite these variations, sufficient similarity in moving from one conservation pattern to another at the same point of time would be found so that the progress of a number of children could easily be plotted on a single graph. As a preliminary step, two graphs were plotted for each child. One showed his total conservation score at each successive interview. The other showed the pattern in which his performance fell at each successive interview.

A variety of attempts to group the individual graphs in some meaningful way highlighted the fact of individual variation. A number of children might be identical in conservation performance at the beginning of the study, and again, at the end of the study. But their progress along the way varied considerably. In the case of children who moved ahead without ever regressing (approximately half of the group in M. C. school), the variations come from the different times at which they moved into patterns 3 and 4. In the case of the other children, additional variation comes from the instances where they performed better at an earlier interview than at a later one.

Table 5-5 shows the number of children in both schools whose performances at the end of the study and at the beginning of the study fell in the same patterns, and within each of these groups, the number of variations in progress. Obviously, the variations also differ from one another.

Table 5-5. Individual Variations from Expected Patterns in
Progress in Conservation

PATTERN OF PERFORMANCE		M. C. SCHOOL		L. C. SCHOOL	
First Interview	Last Interview	Number of Children	Number of Variations	Number of Children	Number of Variations
1	1			1	0
1	2	2	2	11	8
1	3	1	0	2	2
1	4	9	9	2	0
2	2			3	3
2	3	5	5		
2	4	10	6	5	5
3	1	1	0		
3	4	8	4		
4	1	1	0		
4	4	4	2		
Total		41	28	24	18

The significance of the individual variations is apparent when one considers the 31 children in M. C. school whose performances fell in pattern 4, conserving in all three tasks, in the final interview. Of these

31 children, five had conserved in all three tasks at all of the previous interviews; nine had conserved in all three tasks at three previous interviews; six had conserved at two prior times. However, five of the 31 children had conserved in three tasks only once before, and for six of them, the final interview marked the first time for such a performance.

It seems likely that children who have been relatively systematic, or in Piaget's terms "operational," in their thought over a period of one and a half or two years are rather differently oriented to instruction than are their more recently conserving peers. They may have classified much of the information they have received in different ways and accordingly related it to new information in rather different fashion from those who do not conserve.

Further consideration will be given to the question of individual differences when the children's descriptions and explanations are discussed later in this chapter.

Comparison of longitudinal and cross-sectional groups

Table 5-6 shows the number of children whose performance in the conservation tasks fell in various patterns for the cross-sectional first and second-grade groups, and for the longitudinal group when they were in first- and second-grades. For the purposes of this analysis the longitudinal first-grade group in M. C. school includes all the children who remained in the study for three interviews. The longitudinal group in the L. C. school includes, for the first grade, all children who had been interviewed three times and who were classified as adequate in language by the third interview, and, for the second grade, all children who had been interviewed five times and were classified as adequate in language by the fifth interview. We assumed that these children whose language status changed as the study proceeded did not differ in language ability from their first- and second-grade counterparts in the cross-sectional study.

The performances of the longitudinal group in M. C. school are obviously superior at the second-grade level to the second-grade performances of children interviewed only once. At the first grade, after three interviews, their performances are slightly better than those of their first-grade counterparts who were interviewed once. But these dif-

Table 5-6. Comparison of Groups Interviewed Once with Groups Interviewed Successively: Number of Children Revealing Conservation in Three Tasks[a]

TASKS IN WHICH CHILDREN CONSERVED	FIRST GRADE		SECOND GRADE	
	Cross-sectional	Longitudinal (3rd interview)	Cross-sectional	Longitudinal (5th interview)
M. C. School				
None	4	3	1	1
Only B	18	12	11	3
Both B & A	12	11	14	6
B, A, & C	16	17	24	31
Total	50	43	50	41
L. C. School (Children with adequate language)				
None	5	14	6	1
Only B	15	20	16	24
Both B & A	10	7	4	7
B, A, & C	2	2	8	9
Total	32	43	34	41

[a] Task A: Conservation of the equality of two sets of blocks through two transformations.
  B: Conservation of the number of a set of blocks that have been counted, through two transformations.
  C: Conservation of the equality of two amounts of water through one transformation.

ferences must not be taken at face value since the groups involved differ somewhat on other measures, as described below, and the longitudinal group is also known to have had a somewhat different curriculum.

The picture so far as L. C. school is concerned differs somewhat. The longitudinal group at first-grade level does less well than the cross-sectional. (The discrepancy holds as well for the 24 children who were adequate in language from the beginning of the study. See Table 5-2.) But at second grade the longitudinal group is slightly better.

To establish as fact the possibility that repeated interviews account for whatever superiority of performance is found at the second-grade level, some measure of the similarity of the cross-sectional and longitudinal groups is needed. Most of the evidence indicates that the longitudinal group in M. C. school was brighter than its cross-sectional second-grade counterpart, although not brighter than its first-grade counterpart. On the school-administered Pintner-Cunningham tests, given when the second-grade longitudinal group and second-grade cross-sectional group were in first grade, the mean IQ for the cross-sectional group was 113.65, standard deviation 15.17; for the longitudinal, mean 120.80, standard deviation 20.25. The Stencil Design tests, and the Ammons Full-Range Picture Vocabularly tests, individually administered when the cross-sectional group was in second grade and the longitudinal group in kindergarten, do not provide directly comparable data. However, the means of raw scores from the Ammons of 25.06, standard deviation 4.81 and from the Stencil of 3.54, standard deviation 2.42 would indicate that the longitudinal group was advanced at least a year over the norms for the kindergarten. In contrast, the means of the raw scores for the cross-sectional group of 29.72, standard deviation 5.92, and 5.92, standard deviation 2.85, are average for second grade.

Mental ages, based on the Pintner-Cunningham IQ's were computed for both groups. The differences in the distributions for the two groups suggest that the superior performance of the longitudinal group could be related to the greater number of children who were advanced in mental age. To check on this possibility a sample was drawn from the cross-sectional group of all children who could be matched in MA and sex to children in the longitudinal group. Eighteen children were found, matched exactly for mental age, except for two cases where there was a one-month discrepancy. Table 5-7 shows the results, and, while the numbers are too small to be conclusive, suggests that something other than mental age contributes to the superior performance of the longitudinal group. Perhaps the crucial factor rests in the innovations in the mathematics program acting in combination with mental age.

Table 5-7. Number of Children Matched for Sex and Mental Age
Revealing Conservation in Three Tasks in Second Grade

TASKS IN WHICH CHILDREN CONSERVED	GROUP	
	Cross-sectional	Longitudinal
None	0	0
Only B	3	1
Both B & A	7	4
B, A, & C	8	13

Comparison of middle and lower class groups

Throughout the study, the results from the children attending L. C. school have been taken much more tentatively than those from M. C. school. There are two main reasons for viewing the data from the lower class group with considerable caution. The interviewers were often uncertain as to whether the children really understood what was expected from them in the way that the middle class group did, even when they were not conserving. Further, the population in L. C. school was sufficiently mixed that it would be hard to specify whether the children's handicaps should be attributed to language confusions, lack of intellectual stimulation in their homes, cultural deprivation, or some combination of these and other factors.

As in the cross-sectional study, what is most obvious is the discrepancy in performance between the M. C. and L. C. groups. As Table 5-2 indicates, the point at which a quarter of the children are conserving in all three tasks comes about a year later for the L. C. group than it does for the M. C. group. But equally interesting is the fact that the sequence of progress appears so very similar for the two groups. One can speculate that were data available for the third grade they would resemble those for the second grade in M. C. school. On the other hand, the rate of increase, from 4 per cent in the fall of first grade to 25 per cent in the spring, in the number of children who are conserving in all three tasks is not maintained as they move into the second grade. Paralleling this slow movement from conservation in only two tasks to conservation in three tasks is the relatively slow progress made from no conservation to conservation in the easiest task. By second grade 58 per cent of L. C. children are still unable to conserve in any but the easiest task. This is a larger proportion than was the case for M. C. school in the kindergarten. Perhaps, as was suggested earlier in this chapter, failure to begin to conserve at an early age may be associated with a failure to grasp much that goes on in the classroom and elsewhere. The effects of this inability to think in a systematic fashion about various experiences may be cumulative.

Differences within the L. C. group. As has been indicated, the L. C. group was mixed in ethnic origin. Children with Spanish-speaking background were identified through their names and the fact that their teachers had rated them on their language ability. Since only those who were adequate in language in the first interview were included in the basic longitudinal sample, they constitute a rather selected group. In contrast, the other children included in the sample, with a single exception, included all of the Negroes in the kindergarten who remained in the school through the five interviews.

The data were examined to see whether there were any apparent differences in the children with these different backgrounds. Six of the eight children from Spanish-speaking homes had summed standard scores above the median for the entire group, in contrast to six of the sixteen Negro children who were above the median. Almost none of the Negro children conserved at all initially, while most of the other group conserved in one task. The unknown selective factors involved and the small numbers make any generalization dangerous. The performances of the Negro children in the basic longitudinal group were compared on performance at the final interview with all of the other children who had remained in the study for five interviews. Not all of these other children had been included in the basic longitudinal sample because of their inadequacies in language. The differences in the performances of these two groups are minimal and slightly in favor of the Negroes, all but two of whom conserve in one or more tasks. Similarly, in the cross-sectional study, when the Negro children in all three grades are compared with their peers who are adequate in language, the differences are negligible.

Relationships of conservation to other measures

The cross-sectional study posed the question "Do children who are conserving differ from those who are not conserving, in their performances in other kinds of tests?" This question was also raised in the longitudinal study.

Mean performance for various conservation patterns

The means and standard deviations for each of the mental ability and achievement variables were calculated for each of the four conservation patterns at each successive interview. The results closely parallel those of the cross-sectional study in that the differences between pattern 2 (conservation in task B only) and pattern 3 (conservation in both tasks B and A) are not great. There is, however, a rather steady increase in the size of the means from pattern 1 (no conservation) through patterns 2 and 3 to pattern 4 (conservation in all three tasks). The size of the differences between the means for pattern 1 and those for pattern 4 also tends to decrease as the interviews progress and the children grow older.

Progress in conservation related to other measures

The data of the longitudinal study also permitted posing the question of the relationships between conservation and other measures of mental functioning and achievement in terms of the child's progress toward conservation, relative to his peers. From a practical point of view the question might be phrased, "To what extent does knowledge of a child's progress in conservation provide a teacher with information relevant to his ability to cope with the tasks posed in the classroom?"

The sum of standard scores representing each child's performance in relation to that of his peers in his particular school at five successive interviews was correlated with the other variables. The intercorrelations are presented in Tables 5-8 and 5-9.

The variables related to mental ability or aptitude have been separated from those related to academic achievement. Reading readiness, since it is used as an indicator for beginning instruction, is grouped with the former rather than the latter variables. The conservation measure may be regarded as quite reliable. The tasks on which it was based, although limited in number, maintained a consistent order of difficulty over the successive interviews and with different groups of children. Further, the children's performance in them was consistent over a two-week period. The number of children involved is small, notably so in L. C. school. In the latter school the range of abilities represented by the children's performances in most of the tests is also quite narrow. The school-administered tests, particularly those designed for use in the New York City schools, have a limited range of difficulty, so that the children making the top scores may not have an adequate opportunity to display their best abilities. Some of the tests were administered when the children were still in kindergarten, others when they were in first grade, so the results may have been less reliable than for tests given later.

Despite the constraints in the data there are a number of substantial correlations. The relationships among the mental aptitude variables, and among the achievement variables, and also, as Table 5-10 shows, between these two sets of variables, tend to resemble those found in other studies using similar measures.

Table 5-8. Intercorrelations for Mental Aptitude and Conservation

ITEM	N	1	2	3	4	5	6	7	8	M	SD
M. C. School											
Vocabulary	41	=	.32	.14	.34	−.05	.02	−.09	.25	25.65	5.00
Stencil	41		=	.74	.35	.30	.27	.52	.53	3.60	2.35
Pintner	41			=	.44	.41	.39	.64	.60	120.80	20.50
Reading Readiness	37				=	.20	.27	.47	.53	45.60	4.23
Picture Arrangement	41					=	.25	.41	.22	10.80	3.29
Block Design	41						=	.30	.16	10.56	3.15
Object Assembly	41							=	.50	9.48	2.70
Conservation	41								=		
L. C. School											
Vocabulary	24	=	.38	.11	−.01	−.11	.05	−.08	.09	16.41	3.95
Stencil	24		=	.46	.34	.21	.35	.20	.45	1.25	1.51
Pintner	23			=	.67	.71	.50	.57	.49	106.52	19.94
Reading Readiness	23				=	.49	.24	.49	.39	37.93	6.46
Picture Arrangement	24					=	.32	.62	.49	9.62	3.58
Block Design	24						=	.68	.39	9.12	2.41
Object Assembly	24							=	.50	9.16	2.49
Conservation	24								=		

Table 5-9. Intercorrelations for Achievement and Conservation

ITEM	N	1	2	3	4	M	SD
M. C. School							
Reading Growth	38	=	.04	.41	.37	4.22	.99
Premeasurement	39		=	.16	.26	35.84	2.71
Math Concepts	39			=	.53	32.82	3.51
Conservation	41				=		
L. C. School							
Reading Growth	22	=	.77	.69	.39	2.96	.57
Premeasurement	24		=	.82	.41	33.04	3.67
Math Concepts	24			=	.38	25.14	8.83
Conservation	24				=		

So far as the relationship of the conservation measure to the others is concerned, the number of moderate or substantial correlations suggests that information about a child's progress in conservation does have relevance for his instruction. As was indicated in Chapter 2, the literature provides relatively few instances where measures of conservation ability have been correlated with measures more traditionally used in the schools. Where comparisons are available, results are similar

Table 5-10. Intercorrelations, Mental Aptitude, and Achievement

ITEM	READING GROWTH	PRE- MEASUREMENT	MATH CONCEPTS	CONSERVATION
M. C. School				
Vocabulary	.18	.29	.38	.25
Stencil	.42	.41	.58	.53
Pintner	.35	.36	.57	.60
Reading Readiness	.46	.11	.63	.53
Picture Arrangement	.22	.24	.20	.22
Block Design	.18	.04	.30	.16
Object Assembly	.32	.19	.57	.50
Conservation	.37	.26	.53	1.00
L. C. School				
Vocabulary	.26	.15	−.01	−.09
Stencil	.26	.44	.24	.45
Pintner	.31	.42	.47	.49
Reading Readiness	.54	.56	.62	.39
Picture Arrangement	.42	.45	.55	.49
Block Design	.34	.34	.38	.39
Object Assembly	.40	.38	.50	.50
Conservation	.39	.41	.38	1.00

although the size of the correlations, even where the numbers of children involved are larger than in the present study, is no greater.

Progress in conservation and mental aptitude

In the M. C. school the four measures that bear the closest relationship to progress in conservation are the Pintner, Reading Readiness, Stencil, and Object Assembly. In L. C. school, the Object Assembly, Pintner, Picture Arrangement, Reading Readiness, and the Stencil bear similar relationships to conservation.

The fact that both the Pintner and the Reading Readiness tests show considerable relationship to progress in conservation in both schools suggests an underlying common factor that teachers recognize as "mental maturity." The other measures that bear somewhat similar orders of relationship to conservation in both schools, the Stencil and the Object Assembly, both present the child with tasks that appear to demand little verbal ability other than that involved in comprehending the directions.

The test that was selected as a direct measure of verbal ability, the Ammons Picture Vocabulary test, shows small relationship to progress in conservation, even in the middle class school. The reader will recall that the discriminant function analysis in the cross-sectional study indicated that, in association with the variable of chronological age, performance in the Vocabulary test and in the Stencil test contributed differently to the prediction of conservation in the two schools. When the age range was relatively wide the Vocabulary test augmented the prediction from chronological age for the middle class school, while the Stencil test served similarly but to a lesser degree for the lower class school. With a restricted age range in the longitudinal study and a better measure of conservation, the Stencil relates to conservation in both schools, and the Vocabulary test shows less association.

Correlations with WISC subtests

The results for the subtests of the WISC raise any number of questions for speculation, and underline the need for large scale investigations of the relationships between conservation measures and other measures of mental functioning. Our reasons for including these tests were twofold. We wished to compare the results obtained with the Stencil with other performance tests, and we wanted to include some measures that would not penalize the children from L. C. school for their language handicaps. That we succeeded in the latter is clear from the comparison of the results for the two schools. The interviewers reported that the children in L. C. school were fully at ease and apparently well-motivated throughout their performances in the Picture Arrangement, Block Design, and Object Assembly tests.

Wechsler (1949) has specified that the various subtests of the WISC are not intended to tap separate mental abilities, but rather to reflect intelligence as part of the larger whole that is personality. However, to the extent that the three subtests used in the present study reflect some common factor, as "the ability to visualize a whole structure from its parts" (Hagen, 1952), one would anticipate considerable overlap between performance in these tests and performance in conservation tasks. An important element in the latter appears to be an ability to maintain the notion of a totality or a relationship that can be broken up and then reorganized into its original structure.

The differences in the two schools so far as the Picture Arrangement and Block Design tests are concerned are interesting. However, the size of the samples, and uncertainty about the background variables influencing the L. C. group and about the nature of the abilities tapped by the tests, preclude speculation about the personality and interest factors that may be operative.

Progress in conservation and achievement

The academic achievement measures were school-administered, as were the Pintner-Cunningham tests. Although the content of the tests is different, their format is similar, and they demand that the child use similar procedures such as matching, or marking out the incorrect example. The tests have been specifically designed for the New York City schools so it seems likely that they reflect the emphases of the curriculum fairly well.

Since the conservation tasks deal with various aspects of the child's developing concept of number, one would predict a substantial relationship between progress in conservation and in the two mathematics tests. However, the nature of the two tests is also relevant. The Premeasurement test deals with concepts of size, shape, weight, time, indefinite quantity, place, and distance. The child marks pictures to indicate which of several objects is the longest, large enough to hold another object, in the middle, and so on. The Numerical Concepts test deals with the use of symbols to express one-one correspondence, cardinal numbers to express total groupings, quantitative terms such as "double," ordinal numbers as expression of place in a series, and with simple problems involving addition, subtraction, multiplication, division, and fractional parts. For all of these latter tasks a stable concept of number is essential.

The correlation between the latter test and progress in conservation, particularly for M. C. school conforms to the expectations set forth. The degree of associations between each of the two tests and progress in conservation is very similar in L. C. school, quite different in M. C. school. The M. C. children function almost at the top of the Premeasurement test so that the range of scores is narrow. For the L. C. children the test is perhaps as much a test of verbal as of mathematical ability, and the range of scores is wider than in M. C. school.

The reading growth test, actually a measure of early reading status or achievement, shows, as would be anticipated, a considerably less close relationship with conservation than did the reading readiness measure. Nevertheless the presence of some association underlines the fact that the child's ability to conserve has relevance to a number of aspects of his functioning in the school setting.

Progress in conservation and classroom learning

The correlations between progress in conservation and the various measures of mental aptitude and achievement are substantial enough to indicate that the child's ability to conserve is relevant to the tasks he encounters in the classroom. However, one may ask whether knowledge of whether or not a child conserves provides information sufficiently different from that to be gained from other tests to make it worthwhile to gather it.

Our contention is that the appraisal of whether or not a child is conserving, or more broadly, the extent to which his thinking has become systematic, or, in Piaget's terms, "operational," can be made rather directly by the teacher. Such appraisal would not replace other tests, but would be woven into the fabric of classroom instruction. These ideas have not yet been tried out very extensively. We shall leave further speculation about them to the last chapter in this book.

Subsidiary Findings

As in the cross-sectional study it seemed worthwhile to examine the children's responses in the conservation tasks not only for whatever logic they might display but also for the kinds of descriptions and explanations they offered as they observed the transformations.

Descriptions

The children in the longitudinal study, throughout the successive interviews, when they did not indicate an equivalence for the two sets of blocks or the two amounts of water, described the situation in the same ways as the children in the cross-sectional study. In task B when the blocks are bunched, those that are spread are rather consistently described as "more." The occasional comment that the bunched blocks are "more" comes largely from the L. C. children. In both groups, it is the glass that has "more" water.

Explanations

The explanations offered by the children in the longitudinal study differ from those in the cross-sectional study in only two respects. Similar descriptive and action words are used, but there appears to be a tendency for the children in the longitudinal study to attempt to explain in fuller detail and accordingly to use a greater variety of words. In addition, the explanation "It was the same before" (in contrast to the more convinced "It is the same amount") is used to a much larger extent by the children in the longitudinal study. Such an explanation is often given by a child who indicates in response to the interviewer's initial "What about now?" that there are more blocks in one set than in the other or that there is more water in the glass. These explanations seem to indicate that the child is approaching an understanding of conservation, but has not yet grasped it firmly.

When such explanations are considered along with the many in task A that focus on the fact that the blocks have been moved, it appears that a considerable number of children go through a phase of awareness that the equivalence can be restored. Such a finding adds support to the conclusion reached by Wallach and Sprott (1965). They find that training in making such restorations is effective in shifting nonconserving children toward conserving responses. Presumably such training helps the child to think through the consequences of a notion that, left undisturbed, he might hold but never test.

Explanations offered by individuals at successive interviews. The discussion of individual variation in progress toward conservation earlier in this chapter indicated that in the case of about half the children there was some degree of vacillation from conserving to nonconserving responses from one interview to the next. The discussion of the children's explanations in the preceding chapter emphasized that the words used in the explanations did not appear to reflect any systematic approach so far as the children were concerned. Our study of the explanations given in the successive interviews of the longitudinal study tends to reinforce this impression. To give the reader some idea of the data from which these impressions are derived, the successive explanations of several children are presented in Table 5-11. The selections have been made to show variation in both conservation patterns and kinds of explanations.

Sex differences

Despite the fact that no differences were found when boys and girls were compared in their performances in the conservation tasks in the cross-sectional study, it seemed worthwhile to examine the longitudinal data for possible differences in the age at which the concept became relatively stable, or for greater variation during the period of acquisition. The data did not reveal any such differences.

Summary

The results of the longitudinal study confirmed those of the cross-sectional and underlined the relevance of the child's progress in conservation to his performance in the classroom.

The order of difficulty for the conservation tasks held in the longitudinal study as it had for the cross-sectional. However, the longitudinal study highlighted the transitional nature of the age period from five through seven. As Piaget has indicated, during these years a child may give some evidence of understanding conservation but fail to maintain the concept when he is questioned about it or when the circumstances change in some way. Since the questions posed to the children in the present study were not intended to probe suspect answers, the amount of variation is perhaps less than in the more clinical kind of interview. Despite this, about half the children, at least at one point in the series of interviews, "regressed" from what had appeared to be an understanding of conservation at an earlier period.

While the correlations between progress in conservation and other measures of mental aptitude and school achievement were only moder-

Table 5-11. Explanations Offered at Successive Interviews

CHILD	SCHOOL	INTER-VIEW	CONSER-VATION PATTERN	TASK	EXPLANATION
139	M. C.	1	4	A	(Same[a]). *You didn't take them out.*
				C	(Same). *That's* (bowl) *wider. They're same.*
		2	4	A	(Same). *You didn't take away none.*
				C	(Same). *Glasses are the same but bowl is wider. Water spreads out a little more.*
		3	4	A	(Same). *They're still in the line and if you put them in a bunch they'll still be the same amount.*
				B	(Same). *It's still the same amount of water. It just looks more cause it's under that.*
		4	4	A	(Same). *Even though put in pile didn't take any away.*
				C	(Same). *Even though this* (bowl) *is wider this was the same as this* (glasses) *so this* (bowl) *must be the same as this.*
		5	4	A	(Same). *Even though they are in different order, still the same amount.*
				C	(Same). *Even though it's wider it looks like more water but it's still the same amount.*
146	M. C.	1	2	A	*This is in a circle and this isn't, it's around like this.*
				C	*It's much bigger.*
		2	3	A	(Same). *Some are like this and some like that.*
				C	*It's a glass and this one is a bowl. Glass is longer and bowl is shorter.*
		3	4	A	(Same). *The red ones are here and the yellow ones are over here. Same red ones and same yellow ones.*
				C	(Same). *Because this one is more high and this one is more rounder.*
		4	2	A	(More yellow. Asserts twice). *The red aren't straight and the yellow are.*
				C	(More here). *'Cause round is flat and the glass is straight.*
		5	4	A	(Same). *One is just straight and one is round.*
				C	(Same). *'Cause you didn't pour anything back in the pitcher.*

Table 5-11 (continued)

CHILD	SCHOOL	INTER-VIEW	CONSER-VATION PATTERN	TASK	EXPLANATION
121	M. C.	1	3	A	(Same[a]). *All the blocks are on the table.*
				C	*This glass* (empty), *cause this is wider cause it's closed in.*
		2	3	A	(Same). *You just moved them in a different place.*
				C	*This is fatter, can hold more water and it is small.*
		3	3	A	(Same). *You didn't take none away.*
				C	*This has a lower amount of water and this has higher.*
		4	2	A	*More yellow, cause there's no red.*
				C	*This is fatter and this holds more.*
		5	4	A	(Same). *You didn't take any away.*
				C	*Both the same. But the other is just a little fatter.*
429	L. C.	1	2	A	*I don't know.*
				C	*This one is little and that one is big.*
		2	2	A	(No explanation).
				C	*This* (bowl) *is a little glass and that's bigger.*
		3	3	A	(Same). *All of them are together.*
				C	*This bowl is big and that glass is little.*
		4	2	A	*You making them different—more yellows—cause that is like that and these are round.*
				C	*This is the more fatter glass and this is the more skinny.*
		5	2	A	*This* (yellows) *look like this and reds are off the line.*
				C	*This one is skinnier and this one is fatter and this one is fat so this one is a little higher.*

[a] *Same* indicates that the child, in responses prior to the explanation, had indicated that the amounts were the same.

ately high, they were substantial enough and consistent enough to warrant further investigation of the understanding of conservation, and of other manifestations of operational thought as they may relate to the curriculum for the child in kindergarten, first, and second grade.

CHAPTER 6

Children's ideas
about floating objects

THE EMERGENCE of concrete operations at around the age of seven is reflected not only in concepts of conservation but also in children's responses to a variety of other kinds of problems—problems which call for classifying and ordering a number of objects on the basis of various attributes. Piaget has used the problem of floatation in this way (Inhelder & Piaget, 1958). In his investigation, subjects were presented with a collection of disparate objects (stones, wooden blocks, nails, etc.) and were asked to classify them according to whether they float or sink. They were also asked for explanations of their predictions and were encouraged to experiment with the objects and to summarize their findings.

Piaget reports that, although five- and six-year-olds can sort the objects according to predicted action in water, their classifications are not coherent. They are satisfied with multiple, contradictory explanations. Thus some objects are said to float because they are little (or light) and others to float because they are big (or heavy). In some instances a single type of explanation is offered for contrasting predictions; thus, a wooden block floats "because it is heavy" and a rock sinks for the very same reason. Concerning this stage, Piaget concludes, ". . . bodies float or sink equally well if they are large, small, heavy, or light (or even, by association, because they are round, long, etc.)" (Inhelder & Piaget, 1958, p. 28).

Seven- to nine-year-old children, although unable to formulate a concept of density or specific gravity, try to reconcile some of the contradictions inherent in explanations based on absolute weight and volume. They attempt to make ". . . a double entry classification with reference to weight and volume which gives four possibilities: the small light objects, the small nonlight objects, the large light, and the large heavy" (Inhelder & Piaget, 1958, p. 30). The child of this age, according to Piaget, is beginning to revise his notion of weight and ". . . to place the concept of absolute weight . . . in opposition to a new concept of weight perceived as relative to the matter under consideration . . ." (p. 30). These subjects, unlike the younger ones, attempt to coordinate prediction and explanation; and their reference to weight and volume is more systematic.

The results of our pilot studies indicated that the floatation problem was a good one for subjects in the kindergarten and primary grade age range. While it is a complex problem, it is also a problem with which the children are familiar; they respond to it readily, with predictions and explanations. Pilot studies also indicated that older subjects, as Piaget reports, approached the problem in a more systematic way. It also appeared, however, that in some ways they were poorer predictors than the younger subjects. For example, older subjects, using a generalization that large (and/or heavy) objects sink, tended to classify, incorrectly, a block of wood as nonfloating. Younger subjects, perhaps because they were less systematic, seemed to be better predictors on such an item; wood could float for any one of a variety of reasons ("big," "heavy," "light," "because it's wood"). It seemed too that when children were retested after an interval of a few weeks (for reliability purposes) those who were predicting on the basis of some systematic generalization were apt to persist with an erroneous prediction. Thus, the wood would sink "because it's heavy"; some subjects even claimed that "it sank last time." The attempt to construct a coherent classification not only led to certain erroneous predictions but perhaps interfered with accommodation to the observed, but unexpected, action of certain objects.

The Present Study

A number of reasons led to the decision to include a floatation problem in the cross-sectional and longitudinal studies of conservation. An experiment of assured interest to the children seemed necessary as a buffer between the conservation tasks involving the blocks and the task involving the liquid. More importantly we were looking for manifestations (in a situation less structured than the usual aptitude or achievement test) of the logical abilities, or, in Piaget's terms, "operations," that are more explicitly reflected in the conservation tasks. Also, we sought a problem that would bear close resemblance to those that a child might encounter in those aspects of the curriculum where he is encouraged to share his ideas with the other children, in a somewhat informal discussion.

The procedure that was formulated stands somewhere between Piaget's "clinical technique" and a standardized series of questions. The interviewers followed a standard procedure and recorded responses in a standard fashion but there was provision for considerable flexibility. The questions could be modified, in order to follow certain clues provided by the children, and the children were permitted (and encouraged) to manipulate the objects freely and to talk about them at length if they wished. While this kind of flexibility yields interesting data, they are also less reliable than are other kinds. Accordingly the findings must be interpreted cautiously.

With these limitations in view, the floatation study dealt with developmental changes in the accuracy of the children's predictions, the objects they group together, and the attributes they use in their explanations.

Procedures

The interview. For this section of the interview a large oblong plastic container nearly filled with water was placed nearly in front of the child. The interviewer showed the child a plastic boat and a large (two inches in diameter) pebble. The child was asked what he thought would happen when each was placed in the water. This section of the interview was intended to elicit the terms the child used for describing the phenomena of floating and sinking. The child was then given the objects to put in the water.

Following this, the interviewer put on the table, in a standard order, two pieces of wood, one a rectangle approximately two inches by four inches, the other a two-inch square; two wooden toothpicks; two nails slightly shorter than the toothpicks; two pebbles, one slightly smaller than the one used in the initial demonstration, the second considerably smaller. The child was then asked to pick out the ones he thought would "float," or "stay on top," those that he thought would "sink" or "go to the bottom." His initial sorting was recorded, and in the cases where he did not include all the objects, he was asked to predict for them. After his prediction had been made, but before he put the objects in the water, he was asked to state why he thought that each of the objects would behave as he had predicted.

After the explanations for all the objects were recorded, and the child had put them in the water, the interviewer brought out a two-inch paraffin ball and a plasticene ball of identical size and shape, getting the child's prediction and explanation for each. Then a small piece of plasticene was broken from the plasticene ball and a prediction and explanation obtained for that. The child then tested the three objects by putting them in the water.

Analysis of the data. Each child's protocol was scored for the correctness of his predictions and categorized as to the objects he classified as "floating" or "sinking." The attributes he mentioned in his explanations were also categorized.

Results

The cross-sectional study, involving larger numbers of children, has been the major source of the analyses presented here.

Prediction

There are no significant differences in mean prediction scores between the two schools in the cross-sectional study. As Table 6-1 indi-

Table 6-1. Floatation: Mean Prediction Scores[a]
Children from Two Schools (Cross-sectional Study)

GRADE	M. C. SCHOOL		L. C. SCHOOL	
	N	M	N	M
Kindergarten	52	4.77	31	5.19
First	50	5.56	31	5.61
Second	50	5.36	31	5.90

[a] Scores based on initial predictions for nine objects.

cates, what differences do appear seem to favor the children in L. C. school.

As represented in Table 6-1, the differences between grades, in mean prediction, are not pronounced. However, when prediction scores for each of the nine objects are considered separately, some age trends seem evident (Table 6-2). For some objects, accuracy of prediction improves with age, for others there is a decline, and for some there is no clear trend. In Piaget's accounts, older subjects (seven to nine years) attempt to use, in systematic fashion, generalizations such as "light objects float and heavy ones sink," or "small objects float, light ones sink." In the present study the second-grade subjects were the most successful, in prediction, on the three objects (rock, toothpick, clay ball) for which such size/weight generalizations could be expected to lead to correct prediction. Conversely, they were the least successful on items (wood blocks and paraffin) for which such generalizations might lead to erroneous predictions.

Table 6-2. Per Cent of Subjects in Each Grade Giving Correct Predictions on Nine Items (M. C. and L. C. Schools Combined)

ITEM	KINDERGARTEN ($N = 83$)	FIRST GRADE ($N = 81$)	SECOND GRADE ($N = 81$)
Rock	63	81	95
Toothpick	69	67	84
Clay ball	38	57	72
Pebble	52	69	69
Clay piece	63	76	65
Nail	32	43	42
Rectangular wood	59	63	46
Square wood	64	54	44
Paraffin	53	47	40

Sorting and prediction

At the beginning of the floatation section of the interview, subjects were presented with a collection of objects and asked to sort them as floating or sinking, prior to placing them in water. An additional analysis was made of the predictions represented by sortings of these six initial items (considering the two pairs of identical toothpicks and nails as single "items" each).

Phi coefficients in Table 6-3 reflect the fact that first-grade subjects were most likely to be consistent, in sorting, in distinguishing between a relatively large and heavy item (e.g. the square of wood) and small objects. Thus, many of them classed the small objects as floating and the wood as nonfloating; while a number of others made precisely the opposite sort. In either case, such groupings necessarily involved prediction errors (e.g. distinguishing between wood and toothpick,

Table 6-3. Correlation (Phi Coefficients) between Predictions
for Certain Pairs of Objects (M. C. School)

OBJECTS	KINDERGARTEN	FIRST GRADE	SECOND GRADE
Wood (sq.) & toothpick	−.06	−.34[a]	−.31[a]
Wood (sq.) & nail	−.01	−.32[a]	−.45[a]
Wood (sq.) & pebble	−.01	−.43[a]	−.07
Toothpick & nail	.43[a]	.63[a]	.22
Toothpick & pebble	.26	.47[a]	.08
Pebble & nail	.39[a]	.57[a]	.38[a]

[a] p < .05

or grouping toothpick and nail together). Evidence of such groupings was less marked for second grade. A number of these older children began to make correct distinctions between the toothpick and nail and pebble as indicated by the lower, although positive, coefficients. The rock and second wood block are omitted from Table 6-3. The former item, a generally easy one, was not highly correlated with other items. Coefficients for the latter were similar to those shown for the square of wood. A similar pattern of coefficients held for L. C. subjects. The first-grade group had the greatest number of significant coefficients and the kindergarten the least.

When prediction scores representing the sorting of the initial six items are examined, there is evidence that such scores are inversely related to performance on conservation tasks. As shown in Table 6-4, with the exception of the M. C. school first-grade group, "better" conservers tended to be poorer predictors. It is possible that children who handle the conservation tasks well are more likely to approach the sorting task in a more systematic fashion and to use size or weight generalizations that lead to errors in prediction.

Table 6-4. Performance on Conservation Tasks and Mean Prediction Scores
for Initial Set of Six Items

CONSERVATION PATTERN	KINDERGARTEN		FIRST GRADE		SECOND GRADE	
	N	M	N	M	N	M
M. C. School						
1 & 2	37	3.51	22	3.82	12	3.83
3 & 4	15	2.87	28	3.82	38	3.66
L. C. School						
1 & 2	29	3.59	19	3.89	20	4.20
3 & 4	2	2.00	12	3.50	11	3.73

Explanation

Initially, eleven categories were used in classifying explanations. The categories were based directly on the kinds of attributes referred to by subjects; no attempt was made to judge the appropriateness or sophistication of their responses. Upon subsequent analysis, some of the categories were combined, yielding three major types of explanations: weight, dimension, and material. Weight explanations involve descriptions of the objects as light or heavy. Dimension refers to explanations concerning size (big/little) and also to the less frequent explanations of shape and length. Most of the explanations concerning material refer explicitly to the material of which the object is composed. Also included are the less explicit references, "It's like stone," or, naming responses, "It's a nail, nails sink." The latter were not as common as the clearer references to material; when they did appear they were more likely to be associated with material explanations than with those of weight and dimension. Explanations not falling in these three categories were classified as miscellaneous.

As indicated in Table 6-5, the proportion of weight explanations increased with age, and dimensional explanations decreased. The use of material explanations shows little change. Table 6-5 and Table 6-6 show proportions of the total number of explanations given by subjects within a grade. The children were asked to explain each of their predictions; for each grade there was an average of about nine responses per child, with the exception of the kindergarten group in L. C. school where there was an average of four and one-half explanations per child.

Despite the increasing use of weight explanations with age, it is also

Table 6-5. Number of Types of Explanations Used in Different Grades

GRADE	N	WEIGHT	DIMENSION	MATERIAL	MISC.	TOTAL
M. C. School						
Kindergarten	52	140	123	118	70	451
First	50	242	146	93	9	490
Second	50	253	61	142	26	482
L. C. School						
Kindergarten	31	0	98	20	22	140
First	31	77	82	94	17	270
Second	31	155	53	61	9	278

evident that such responses are negatively related to prediction scores. As shown in Table 6-6, children with low prediction scores make the greatest use of weight explanations while those with high scores refer to weight much less frequently. The scores have been combined into three groups, high, middle, and low.

Table 6-6. Prediction Score and Number of Types of Explanations Used (Grades Combined)

PREDICTION SCORE	N	WEIGHT	DIMENSION	MATERIAL	MISC.	TOTAL
M. C. School						
High (9, 8, 7)	51	165	132	190	35	522
Middle (6, 5)	63	245	139	117	48	549
Low (4, 3, 2)	38	225	59	46	22	352
L. C. School						
High (9, 8, 7)	39	74	125	111	3	313
Middle (6, 5)	36	84	60	60	32	236
Low (4, 3, 2)	18	74	48	4	13	139

Material explanations, on the other hand, appear positively associated with prediction scores. Grades are combined in Table 6-6. Inasmuch as the three grades did not differ markedly in mean prediction score, they have, roughly, equivalent representation in the prediction groups in Table 6-6. Although not shown above, the association between prediction score and type of explanation also holds true when each grade is treated independently. It should be noted as well that the difference between high and low predictors cannot be attributed to reticence, on the part of one of the groups, in offering explanations. In both schools, for all grades the high and the low predictors averaged slightly more explanations per child than did the middle group.

Prediction and explanation—longitudinal study

Mean prediction scores for the five interviews of children in the longitudinal group are shown in Table 6-7. By the fifth interview (the middle of the second grade) the average scores of these subjects was about one point higher than the average of the second-grade subjects in the cross-sectional groups.

Table 6-7. Mean Prediction Scores of Longitudinal Group

INTERVIEW	M. C. SCHOOL	L. C. SCHOOL
1st	4.66	5.20
2nd	5.49	5.80
3rd	6.24	6.62
4th	7.02	6.71
5th	7.07	6.87

Table 6-8 shows that there was general improvement in prediction on all items up to the third interview. For a number of items, improvement thereafter was not marked. When the data in Tables 6-7 and 6-8

Table 6-8. Per Cent of Subjects in Longitudinal Interviews Giving Correct Predictions on Nine Items (M. C. and L. C. Schools Combined; $N = 65$)

	INTERVIEW				
ITEM	1	2	3	4	5
Rock	69	71	86	77	83
Toothpick	69	65	66	74	89
Clay ball	35	55	71	60	68
Pebble	49	54	71	89	83
Clay piece	58	75	74	85	85
Nail	32	49	66	72	72
Rectangular wood	55	72	80	88	81
Square wood	65	65	71	81	72
Paraffin	52	54	54	65	69

are compared to findings in the cross-sectional study, it is evident that experience in the interviews contributed to accuracy in prediction. It should be noted, however, that despite general increases in accuracy, there was considerable fluctuation in the scores of individuals. Thus, for 24 of the 65 children, scores on the second testing (mean of 6.6) were equivalent to or higher than their scores on the fifth testing (mean of 6.0). Similarly, there was a decline of two or more points for fourteen subjects when scores on the fourth and fifth interviews are compared. Apparently, the floatation problem, in terms of prediction, continued to be a difficult one for many subjects throughout the five interviews.

In Table 6-9, the explanations of the better predictors (scores of

Table 6-9. Prediction Score and Number of Types of Explanation Used: Fifth Interview, Longitudinal Group

| PREDICTION SCORE | N | EXPLANATION | | | | |
		WEIGHT	DIMENSION	MATERIAL	MISC.	TOTAL
M. C. School						
(9, 8)	18	73	15	93	7	188
(7 & lower)	23	145	53	35	16	249
Combined	41	218	68	128	23	437
L. C. School						
(9, 8)	12	19	45	62	9	135
(7 & lower)	13	55	70	22	2	149
Combined	25	74	115	84	11	284

8 or 9) are compared with those of poorer predictors, on the fifth and final interview. The distribution of explanations of the M. C. group as a whole ("Combined" in Table 6-9) is very similar to that of the cross-sectional second grade reported in Table 6-5. This close resemblance is not found when the L. C. group as a whole is compared to the parallel cross-sectional group. Of greater interest is the fact that despite some general differences between the longitudinal and cross-sectional groups in prediction and explanations, a similar association between prediction score and type of explanation is found in both groups. Thus in the longitudinal group, as in the cross-sectional, weight explanations are more commonly used by poorer predictors and material

by the better predictors. This association, shown in Table 6-9 for the fifth interview, was evident in the preceding interviews of the longitudinal group as well.

Summary

In general, the results of the floatation study tend to support the analysis of the problem made by Piaget. However, the age range in the present study is too narrow for adequate testing of all of his theoretical formulations.

The accuracy of a child's prediction of the behavior of a given object when placed in water appears to be related to the extent to which his generalizations from his experiences with objects of varying size and weight are relevant. Accordingly, children who are conserving, and consequently approaching in a systematic way the task of sorting objects into floating and sinking classes, are likely to make less accurate predictions than children who are not conserving and are presumably responding more randomly or on the basis of memory.

The results in this study parallel the results in the conservation studies in a number of ways. The trends with chronological age are similar. There are differences between the two schools, but as in the other studies, these differences are related to the nature of the tasks. Of most importance, there are indications of the different ways that children in the same grade view phenomena and problems that the adult regards as similar or even identical. The significance of such diversity for the early childhood curriculum and for the instruction of the child remains to be explored.

CHAPTER 7

Theoretical issues and educational implications

THE STUDIES reported here have dealt with two major questions. The first question had to do with the validity of Piaget's description of the development of understanding of the principle of conservation. The second had to do with the relevance of such understanding to children's progress and achievement in kindergarten, first, and second grade. The results of the studies support Piaget's findings and underline the educational importance of the understanding of conservation.

The children's performance in the conservation tasks in the longitudinal as well as in the cross-sectional study fell into patterns indicating a similar sequence in the attainment of understanding of conservation. This sequence also held for children in schools in different neighborhoods. But the progress from one level of understanding to the next was considerably slower for the children who came from the lower class background.

The consistency of findings insofar as the sequence is concerned underscores the importance of maturational factors in the child's ability to conserve and, more generally, in the transition from thought that is intuitive and perceptually dominated to thought that is systematic, or, in Piaget's terms, "operational." But the findings also highlight the role of experiential factors and, more specifically, raise the question of how the transition from one level of thought to another may be brought about. This question has theoretical interest for both the psychologist and the educator.

In the first section of this chapter we re-examine the question of sequence and transition, considering some of the limitations in our studies and the issues that continue to demand investigation. In later sections of the chapter, making the assumption that Piaget's theories regarding the nature of intellectual development in the early childhood period are quite tenable, we turn to the implications that can be drawn for teaching young children, and for the curriculum to be provided.

Sequence and Transition

Summaries of the major findings of the present studies are to be found at the ends of Chapters 4, 5, and 6 and need not be repeated here. However, before discussing the issues that arise from them, it may be appropriate to remind the reader of some of the ways the treatment of the data differs from that reported by Piaget.

In most of his descriptions of the development of the understanding of conservation, Piaget writes of three stages: an initial period in which there is no conservation; a period of transition in which the child sometimes appears to conserve but changes his assertion momentarily depending on the extent of the transformation he confronts; finally, a period when he appears to be completely convinced and logical.

In the present studies the sequence of development has been described in terms of the number of children who were able to conserve in each of three tasks in kindergarten, first grade, and second grade. Transition has been a matter of moving from conservation in no task, to conservation in a task involving counting, and later to conservation in this same task plus conservation in a number task not involving counting, and finally to conservation in both these two plus a task involving the conservation of an amount of liquid.

The three conservation tasks used in the present studies illustrate certain aspects of Piaget's approach, but they are hardly representative of the intricacies of his method. Nor do the tasks of the present study reflect adequately the complex interrelationships that he postulates must obtain among the abilities involved in conservation, in classification, and in seriation before the child is truly logical or operational in his thinking. There is some indication that performance in the floating task involving classification and in the stairs task, a task calling to some extent on ordering or seriation abilities, follows trends similar to those found in the conservation tasks. But much further investigation is needed to verify the nature of the development of each of these abilities and the processes that underly their eventual association into a coherent system.

Maturation and experience

The findings of the present studies indicating that increasing chronological age is associated with increased success in the conservation tasks, and that the sequence of the development of the abilities represented in the tasks is the same in both schools, highlight the importance of maturational factors. But the difference between the two schools, and the differences between the results for the cross-sectional and longitudinal groups in the middle class school, suggest that within whatever limits may be set by maturational factors, experience also contributes importantly.

One might argue that the ordering of success in the tasks is dependent on the children's experience with counting, which would be most directly applicable in the two tasks involving the sets of blocks. Piaget, however, maintains that there is no connection between the ability to count and the logical operations used in maintaining the equivalence of two sets of objects. It is true that the easiest task in the present study was the one where the child had the opportunity to count the number of blocks in the set before its configuration changed. But the ability to count was very often not brought to bear in the task involving the conservation of the equivalence of the two sets of blocks. This was true even when the standard order of presentation of the tasks was changed so that the child had the opportunity to conserve after counting prior to being posed the task in which counting was not suggested.

While rote counting may contribute little to the ability to conserve, other kinds of experience may have more direct relevance. Piaget's work would suggest that children who have had many opportunities to classify objects on the basis of similar properties, or to order along dimensions of difference, or better, opportunities of both kinds, might arrive at the level of operational thought represented in conservation sooner than children who have not had such opportunities. In this connection, it is interesting that most of the training studies reported in the literature to date have worked with what seem to be the elements immediately involved in the conservation task, such as addition and subtraction or reversibility, rather than with what may well be the developmentally prior abilities of classifying and ordering. More recently, judging from informal reports, some investigators have become interested in training procedures directed toward improving these latter abilities. The children are reported to be enthusiastic abut the various games and devices that have been tried, and there is some indication that progress toward and understanding of conservation may be facilitated in this fashion. But there are a number of possibilities that must be considered in evaluating the effectiveness of any measure designed to promote such intellectual progress.

"Matching" the child's conceptual level. We have speculated that the superior performance of the longitudinal group in the middle class school might stem from the innovations in the mathematics program in combination with the good mental ability of the children. Had there been a less able comparison group who had had similar experience with the Cuisenaire materials in kindergarten and the Suppes program in first and second grade, we suspect their performances in the conservation tasks might not have been as good as were those of this rather bright group. Our contention is that the success of the various "new" programs in mathematics, and presumably in other areas of the curriculum as well, is largely dependent on their appropriateness for the conceptual abilities of the children receiving instruction. This point of view is also supported by various experimental studies dealing with children's conceptual abilities, particularly as they relate to conservation.

Rather consistently so far, training procedures of whatever kind have been most successful with children who gave some indication of being in a transitional stage in the pretraining measures. In Piaget's terms one might say that such a child is already accommodating his thought to the logic of the adult, while the training offers him the opportunity to assimilate the ideas into his own repertoire. If the latter has really occurred, the child can be expected to demonstrate his understanding with different materials and in differing social contexts. On the other hand, if the responses demanded in the training are too remote from those already in the child's repertoire, there may be neither accommodation nor assimilation, or an accommodation to the demands of the training procedure without any transfer to new situations or new materials. Under these circumstances such training might more effectively be postponed until there is closer correspondence between the expectations set for the child's performance and his ability to comprehend what is wanted from him.

This is not to say that in the meantime the child is necessarily better left to his own devices, although Piaget's theory clearly carries the implication that the young child has as much, if not more, to learn from his own active encounters with his physical environment and from his exchanges with his peers as he has from the adult. But adults, parents, and teachers, to say nothing of psychologists attempting to unravel cognitive processes, are constantly responsible for decisions that determine the nature of the child's encounters and exchanges. The parent and the teacher, with generally more extensive opportunities for observing the child's interests and responses in a wider variety of situations, are, at least potentially, in a better position to provide challenge appropriate to his developing abilities than is the psychologist in the typical experimental situation.

The fact that so many children without instruction directed toward the eventual understanding of conservation nevertheless come to grasp the idea around the age of seven, or even before, has been used to argue that such an understanding is a natural outcome of the child's living in a social environment. But the number of children who fail to reach such understanding, and the evidence that faulty logic underlies many of the misconceptions of both older children and adults argues in favor of giving deliberate attention to whatever underpinnings of logical thought can be identified in the early childhood period. Piaget's theory suggests that the search for these should be focused at least as much on the child's activities with physical objects as on his verbalizations.

The role of language. The findings of the present studies suggest that middle class children early acquire sufficient vocabulary to describe their own observations and manipulations reasonably well. A study dealing with the classification abilities of kindergarten and second-grade children currently in progress suggests that they readily identify by name such properties of objects as size, shape, color, texture, material, and so on. But such verbal identification is no guarantee that the properties will be used consistently in a sorting task. In contrast to this there is some indication in the floatation studies that the children from disadvantaged homes had less difficulty in sorting than they did in making verbal identification of the properties. Training designed to increase the appropriate vocabulary might considerably facilitate the later development of logical thinking for these children. Whether similar training would be equally effective for children who are already well advanced verbally is less clear.

Matching the child's conceptual "style." The differences between the middle and lower class groups may also be matters of cognitive "style." The good predictions of the lower class children in the floatation problem may have been based on their associations from previous experience—"stones go down"—rather than on any awareness of the relevant properties. Their "style" might be termed "relational" in contrast to the more "analytical" approach of their middle class peers.

Such differences in the individual's ways of organizing his environment may show some association with socioeconomic status as current research is beginning to suggest, but longterm longitudinal and other studies (Kagan, Moss, & Sigel, 1963) also underline the importance of these differences among individuals with similar backgrounds. Although there is, to our knowledge, relatively little published research relating Piaget theory to the study of cognitive styles, the relevance of the two lines of experimentation to each other is obvious. There seems little question that most of Piaget's tasks give an advantage to the child who tends to approach his environment analytically, in contrast to the youngster whose approach is more global and associative. Conceivably, it may be the latter kind of child who approaches the level of operational thought more slowly and reverts to a preoperational level more readily. This raises the further question of when and how such a child may provide the adult with clues as to an appropriate match between the repertoire of responses already available to him and the expectations to be set for him in either a training or an educational procedure.

The problem of transition. We come full circle to the problem of the nature of the transition from one level of thought to the next. Piaget (1964) has described the factors he believes to be involved—maturation, social interaction, physical activity, and, more importantly, the process of "equilibration." It is the latter concept that has stimulated interest in the possibilities for matching or pacing the new ideas presented to the child to the level of cognitive development he has already attained. Both experimentation and less formal observation of children provide instances where a child apparently modifies a concept as new information transforms old ideas. But there are few, if any, rules for either the shift from a simple to a more sophisticated concept, or the transition from an intuitive to an operational level of thinking.

Current experimentation is designed to specify some such rules, so far as certain concepts, such as the conservation of substance or number, or class inclusion, are concerned. Pretesting indicates the ideas individual children already hold regarding the specified concept. Training consists of presenting to them what is believed to be the necessary new information in varied ways. Posttesting for the concept yields a measure of the effectiveness of the varied modes of presentation for children of different ages, backgrounds, conceptual levels (and, conceivably, cognitive styles).

While there is no question of the usefulness of experimentation that results in more knowledge of the processes underlying the formation of specific concepts, such experimentation only begins to tackle the problems inherent in the transition from intuitive to operational thought.

Piaget's experiments were ingeniously devised to reveal the presence or absence of certain logical operations in several different areas of knowledge. In some of the current experimentation, the necessity for simplifying difficult problems so the children can grasp their elements has led to such specific training that the possibilities for transfer to related problems in different contexts seem limited. If we understand Piaget correctly, the essence of the concrete operational level of thought is the child's ability to solve a *variety* of problems in a systematic fashion. Consequently, if a child who has undergone a period of training responds correctly in a variety of conservation tasks, but makes illogical mistakes in his mathematics lesson, or fails to understand the class inclusion operation in a classification task, or can only order a series of objects by a manipulative trial-and-error process, he cannot be said to have completed the transition from intuitive to operational thinking.

We detect in some of the reports of experimentation, and in some of the discussions of the possibilities for advancing the child's understanding by matching or pacing his intellectual development, a degree of impatience with the playful, imaginative, highly personalized thought of the young child. We infer that the sooner childish thoughts are put away, the more surely and the more insightfully the person enters into the intellectual kingdom set up for him by the great thinkers in the various disciplines. It is true that when the child reaches the point where he *can* think in a logical systematic fashion, imaginative play begins to decline. Seven- and eight-year-olds tend to be much more matter-of-fact, much less fanciful in their ideas, than are five- and six-year-olds. But the kind of thinking represented in the play of early childhood does not vanish completely when the child reaches the operational level, and it flourishes again in adolescence. Further, there is much in the daydreaming, speculating, and even creative thinking of the adult that resembles the imaginative, intuitive thought of early childhood. Perhaps this kind of thinking so characteristic of the preoperational child bears a relation to the creative, metaphorical thought of the adult, similar to that between the child's concrete operational thought and the adult's formal thought.

Viewed from another direction, the playful and, to the adult, unsystematized thought of the young child may serve to integrate the patterns of action, or, in Piaget's term, schemata, that make up the intellectual repertoire of the infant and toddler. Piaget (1962) has elaborated on this possibility in *Play, Dreams and Imitation*, but this volume appears to have received somewhat less attention from those interested in experimentation than have certain of his other works. It does not deal with specific areas of knowledge, or with their logic, in the same way that his other books do. Further, it is not as easy to derive a program of instruction from it.

The point we wish to emphasize here is that there is no guarantee that instruction in specific concepts will necessarily hasten the transition from one level of thinking to the next. But even if evidence accrues that it does, the question of whether such acceleration, from a long-term view, enhances or stultifies the individual's abilities for speculative, imaginative, even creative thinking still needs investigation.

Implications for the Education of Young Children

From a theoretical view, whatever questions regarding the sequence of intellectual development Piaget's formulations and the experiments related to them have settled, as many more remain to be answered. But for the educator who is faced with the practical problems involved in helping children to grasp certain basic ideas, the theory and, more importantly, the method of Piaget carry immediate and important implications.

The studies reported here have demonstrated the relevance of the ability to conserve to the child's educational progress. Now we turn to some speculation regarding some of the ways the teacher can facilitate the child's progress if he understands the theory and can use the methods of Piaget. Finally, we examine the curriculum for early childhood in the light of Piaget's work.

Teaching the young child

Teachers in kindergarten, first, and second grade, and their colleagues in the middle and upper grades, are often aware that communication with these younger children is somehow more difficult than with the older ones. Piaget's theory suggests that the difference between the two age groups is chiefly a matter of the way they organize and systematize, or, in the case of the younger children, fail to organize systematically, the experiences they have.

Teachers of the younger children with an intuitive, although not necessarily explicit, understanding of this difference tend to organize life in the classroom, the materials they present to the children, and the questions they ask them, in such a way that the children's lack of systematic thought is only occasionally revealed. But when the children are confronted with a problem that demands more than memory or association, a problem that calls for the flexibility and reversibility of operational thought, the limitations in their thinking are apparent.

An example comes from a first-grade teacher, and relates to the teaching of arithmetic. In using a particular workbook, she has found that many children have difficulty at the same point. They have been successfully completing exercises that required them to supply the sums for rows and columns in a series of diagrams. Then comes a set of exercises in which the sums are presented and they must write in the appropriate figures for the rows and columns. The numbers involved are small and the context provided by the diagrams has not changed. Nevertheless, the children who presumably have been relying largely on memory in the previous problems are thoroughly confused. The teacher commented that these children are not yet really "operational" in their thinking. Piaget's analysis helped her to understand the problem as it was viewed by the children. It also led her to question whether these children had had sufficient concrete experience to build a stable concept of number, or whether the earlier exercises had been insufficiently varied.

Piaget's theory does not propose that a child should never be confronted with a problem that may be beyond his comprehension. But it does argue strongly that to permit him to learn an appropriate answer without making certain that he can retrace his steps, or arrive at the same result in another way, is to encourage the erection of a verbal superstructure that may crumble under even minimal cognitive stress.

Crucial as is the teacher's awareness of the young child's mental confusions, no less important is the recognition that he has moved ahead, and is capable of dealing with problems on an operational level. Children are themselves sometimes aware of such important shifts in their own thinking. One seven-year-old, for example, revealed such insight when he commented to his teacher during a mathematics session in which the class had been experimenting with the relationships among containers of various shapes and sizes, "Yesterday we just poured. Today we are really measuring."

Children rarely make such explicit statements of a transition in their thinking and teachers need other means of assessment. Piaget's experiments seem admirably suitable for these purposes.

Assessing the young child's thinking

In addition to many variations of the conservation experiments from which the conservation tasks in the present studies were derived, Piaget's volumes are filled with dozens of experiments designed to reveal the nature of the child's thinking. The experiments, regardless of the conceptual content (number, space, elementary physics, classification, etc.) share certain common elements.

Piaget's experiments. In general, these experiments involve some manipulation of objects or materials on the part of the child. The materials and objects are either of a sort likely to be found (or readily constructed) in any moderately well equipped classroom or in the home kitchen, sewing, or carpentry kit.

Individual approach. As described by Piaget, most of the experiments are carried on with a single child, but there are many possibilities for the teacher to work with several children at the same time. Obviously, since the goal of the experimentation is to furnish information about the thinking of the individual child, whatever procedures are used must insure freedom for each child to reveal his own thoughts, rather than repeating, parrot-like, a response that he suspects is the one the teacher wants.

Method of interrogation. Piaget's way of questioning is intended to guard against such repetition. A suspect answer is carefully probed with other questions, the original question is repeated or rephrased or the materials are manipulated in some way. The method has been criticized on the basis that the child may respond to clues other than those intended by the adult. This criticism seems to us to have more validity for the psychologist interested in normative data and control over as many variables as possible than it has for the teacher whose continuing association with the child permits exploration of his ideas in a variety of circumstances.

The inclination to attribute a child's confusion to the nature of the question is reduced when (as in the present studies) the investigators pose the same question to several hundred children and note that what is apparently confusing to most kindergarteners is crystal clear to most second graders. Our conviction is that the child's responses are shaped not so much by the question put to him, as by his way of looking at the materials and objects in the experiment. This conviction has been further strengthened by a study (begun in 1965) involving children's understanding of class concepts.

In this study, the investigator (Paula Miller) has attempted to teach children the concept of class inclusion. She has worked with kindergarten and second-grade children who are able to sort objects on the basis of a specified attribute such as form, size, or color, but who do not yet understand that a group of objects classified on the basis of one property may include objects that differ in respect to some other property. For example a group, or class, of *metal* cars may include red cars and blue cars, and there are more metal cars than there are red cars or blue cars. The protocols from the informal training sessions are replete with instances where the child's comments indicate that he has turned the adult's questions to his own way of thinking. Illustrative of this tendency is the child who, in response to a question asking him to indicate whether there were more metal or more blue cars, said "more blue." Asked to repeat the investigator's question, he phrased it as, "Are there more blue cars or more red cars?" Another youngster working with a collection of wooden blocks, some green, some yellow, and varied in shape, sorted them according to color and shape, and was then posed the question of whether there was any way they could all be grouped together. She agreed that *all* were made from wood. But to the question of whether they were not then all the same in that way, she responded that this was not possible, for some were green and some yellow. It was apparent that, for her, color was more salient than material, and she could not yet grasp the inclusiveness of the wood category.

While the above illustrations are intended to support our contention that it is the child's perception of the experiment, or his understanding of the concept involved, that shapes his responses, the nature of the questioning ought not be overlooked. The assumption, it should be noted, is not that there is a single correct answer. The focus is not on what is right or wrong, but on what the child believes, and the questions are intended to confront the child's belief from a number of different stances, in order to test its stability.

In his early work, when Piaget had not yet begun to parallel his interrogation with actual experimentation, he wrote that his "clinical method" could only be mastered after some months of training and experience. Piaget's questions, even when associated with experiments, are not the sort typically used most frequently in classroom discourse. Not only beginners, but experienced teachers who are generally skillful in their exchanges with children, may need considerable practice before they become thoroughly adept and insightful in their questioning. But even a somewhat inept beginner and the children with whom he works may derive rather immediate benefits from the experimentation.

We have no statistics from our associations with the teachers of young children, but we have reason to believe that the majority of them, though they may initially find Piaget's ideas difficult, nonetheless sense their relevance to their teaching. Furthermore, those who work through one experiment with one child are not inclined to stop there, and extended experimentation leads not only to better comprehension of Piaget, but more importantly to increased insight into the nature of the learning tasks confronting the children.

The teacher who has mastered Piaget's method has immediately at his fingertips a powerful tool for appraising the child's progress. We do not see it as a tool replacing the more traditional methods of assessment. Standardized intelligence and achievement tests serve purposes for which Piaget's techniques are not suitable. But a well-constructed Piaget interview provides the teacher with something more than he customarily gets from standardized test results. This is a picture of the ways the child organizes (or fails to organize) information. His errors and his misconceptions are revealed *as they occur*. From this direct observation of his functioning in a problem-solving situation, the teacher can derive many clues as to either his readiness for more complex learning or the kinds of experience he may need before he can move ahead. Although many of Piaget's experiments are obviously most relevant to a particular area of the curriculum, the information to be gained from using a given experiment to interview a child is seldom limited to that one experiment but carries implications for the child's performance in other similar tasks.

There seems to be little question that skillful use of Piaget's techniques could greatly enhance the teacher's effectiveness. But it should also be noted that the techniques draw on pedagogical skills that seldom receive much emphasis in teacher preparation. Among these skills are those involved in individual interviewing and the logical analysis of subject matter.

The teacher's preparation. Piaget has indicated that the teacher's preparation should provide an opportunity both to carry through some of the experiments he has devised with children of differing ages and abilities and to design and administer original experiments to test children's understanding of some specified concept. If these ideas were incorporated into preservice preparation, current notions as to an appropriate balance between observation of and participation with groups of children might be revised so as to include more structured interviewing of children. This in turn would necessitate greater emphasis on *listening* to children as opposed to *telling* them, and on the ways the kinds of questions posed to children, whether in the individual interview or in the discourse of the classroom, circumscribe the children's responses.

The current trend to stress the mastery of subject matter in the preparation of all teachers, including those who will work at the youngest levels, might be enhanced by the introduction of some of Piaget's methods. We have been struck by the extent to which adults confronting ideas that are relatively new to them tend to regress from the formal level of thinking of which they are presumably capable, to a concrete operational, and sometimes preoperational, level of thought. It may well be that more explicit recognition of this tendency in the teaching of the teacher, and more insistence that he demonstrate understanding on *both* concrete *and* formal verbal levels, would considerably facilitate his ability to guide the thinking of the children. Such experience might also help him to appraise textbook and other materials from the standpoint of their logical development and consequent degree of difficulty for a particular group of children.

As we indicated in our introduction to this report, we began our studies with the conviction that the curriculum for early childhood education, particularly in the kindergarten, was often woefully lacking in intellectual content. In the years since our project had its inception, this situation has almost reversed itself and the trend now seems to be to view the kindergarten, and even the nursery-school child, as a citizen of an extremely complex world in which the ability to understand and use highly complex and abstract knowledge is essential for meaningful survival. Accordingly, the adequacy of his curriculum is judged on the degree to which it seems to be introducing him to concepts that are believed to be *basic* to such understanding. There is no necessary intent to regard the young child as a potential mathematician, physicist, or economist, although some experimental programs have been subjected to criticism on these grounds. What is essential in all these new programs is that concepts presented be such that the children can learn to grasp them. We can think of no better safeguard against meaningless verbalization and rote memorization than a teacher who is able both to appraise the difficulty of the concepts and to assess the children's comprehension of them. Accordingly, the most important implications of Piaget's work seem to us to lie in its contribution to the teacher's understanding and skill. But it also has some relevance to the curriculum.

The Curriculum for the Young Child

Someone has suggested that Piaget's experiments, in and of themselves, could provide an educational program that would be considerably richer in intellectual content than the traditional program in the kindergarten years. But to limit a program to the activities involved in the experiments would seem to overlook some of the essential tenets of Piaget's theory.

Sequence. Piaget's work clearly implies an ordering among conceptual tasks that suggests certain priorities for instruction. Thus experience in classifying and ordering objects on the basis of a single attribute would presumably precede problems involving the manipulation of two attributes or a relationship between two attributes.

If we understand Piaget correctly, however, the fact that there is an order in the way the child comes to grasp these concepts does not mean that his educational experiences are to be entirely limited to those that are within his immediate understanding. One does not have to wait for evidence that new information has been effectively assimilated before providing opportunity for accommodation to additional information. But neither should the new come so fast as to preclude integration of the old.

As we have indicated earlier, the transitional nature of the early childhood period, and the fact that it is, from Piaget's view, a period when the child is constructing a systematic way of thinking, raises many questions about both the time and the way in which the child responds to the order and the structure that come from the adult. Whether it is variety in experience, or the ordering of experience, or some subtle interaction of the two aspects, that propels the child to operational thought, is not clear. The needed proportions may differ for children of differing backgrounds. In any event, Piaget's theory seems to caution those concerned with curriculum construction to give due attention to the scope or breadth of content and activity as well as to the sequence in which it is presented.

Manipulative activity and language. Piaget's theory leaves no question as to the importance of learning through activity. Demonstrations, pictured illustrations, particularly for the youngest children, clearly involve the child less meaningfully than do his own manipulation and his own experimentation. While the vicarious is certainly not to be ruled out, it is direct experience that is the avenue to knowledge and logical ability.

Language is important, but for Piaget the ability to use language to express logic is an outcome of activity. Attempts to improve the child's logic solely through instructing him in the use of language are not likely to be very successful.

Perhaps the point to be made for those who would construct curriculum is that in the early childhood period activity and language need close association. For example, in the case of the socially disadvantaged child, no adquate comparison of quantities can be made by a child who does not understand the terms "more" and "less," or "most" and "least." But comprehension of those terms may not be developed through words alone, or even associations of word and picture, but rather through a combination of manipulation and verbalization.

Social interaction among children. Piaget parallels the contribution to the child's logical thinking that is made by his physical activity with the contribution that is made by the social exchanges he has with his peers. The latter, he believes, tends to correct the tendency to take an egocentric view of the world. A child may learn more readily from a peer, or a somewhat older child whose views are less distant from his own than are an adult's, than from adult instruction.

The implications to be drawn for curriculum are in part dependent on how Piaget is interpreted. Perhaps Piaget refers chiefly to the informal give-and-take of play, where the child comes rather directly and sometimes painfully against the wishes and desires of other children, and must learn to make allowance for these if he is to gain his own measure of satisfaction. This might suggest that the so-called "free" play that is traditionally included in the kindergarten and sometimes also in the first-grade curriculum has implications for cognitive development quite apart from its intellectual content.

But one might carry Piaget's emphasis on social interaction into the curriculum more directly. For example, small groups of children might be assigned to work together, not, as is so often the case, merely carrying on parallel activities, but actually sharing them. Children who seem to have understood a particular concept might be given opportunities to help children who appear less certain. Perhaps the aim in "grouping" children for various activities within the class should more often be heterogeneity in ability, and less often, the homogeneity that teachers often seek and so seldom find.

Piaget's theory here also carries implications for the grouping of children within the school. The narrow age ranges (usually one year to a grade, but in the case of kindergarten and nursery school sometimes as little as six months) that have been typical, in most schools, may stultify the possibilities for children learning from one another. The ungraded classroom, covering a wider span of years, may offer more possibilities for the children's intellectual expansion.

It should of course be clear that recognition of the importance to the development of logical thought of the child's interaction with his peers does not imply the teacher's abdication from instruction. Unless he sees to it that the children have materials, equipment, *and* ideas, there is no reason to believe that anything of important intellectual value will emerge from their association together.

The role of "discovery." Much has been made of late of the importance of children's finding out, or "discovering," new ideas or new relationships for themselves. From one point of view, this is the essence of Piaget theory—the child comes to an understanding of the world through his own efforts. While he may accommodate his thought to the ideas of others, it is only as he tries those ideas out within the context of the ideas he has previously acquired that he makes them his own.

But there is no reason to believe that a discovery is more meaningful if the child has had to flounder aimlessly for a period before making the discovery. The essence of Piaget's method, it might be said, is the assessment of the child's readiness to make a particular discovery, and the pacing of his educational experience to that readiness so that he will have both the intellectual content and the cognitive abilities needed to make it. There is nothing in either the theory or the method to imply that there is no place for the giving of direct instruction, or for the supplying of organized information. The implication is, rather, that the curriculum should be so arranged as to organize information so that it is within the grasp of the child, once he has sufficient opportunity to explore and manipulate it.

The place of beginning reading instruction. Any discussion of the curriculum for early childhood eventually confronts the question of when instruction in beginning reading is to begin, and whether early instruction is to be direct or incidental to the ongoing activities of the classroom. Piaget, so far as we are aware, has nothing to say about this. However, the findings in our studies of a rather substantial correlation between performance in conservation tasks and progress in beginning reading suggests that, to some extent, similar abilities are involved. A program designed to nurture logical thinking should contribute positively to readiness for reading. This is not to say that the activities that are specific to the development of logical thinking should replace those that are now encompassed under "reading readiness." But there is a need in many programs for a re-examination of the content of the reading readiness program, and of the time allotted to it.

Although specific evidence on this point is not presently available, we suspect that the teacher who has mastered Piaget's techniques will become more diagnostic in his views of all areas of instruction. Accordingly, he may become much more skillful in pacing instruction in reading and writing skills to the individual child's apparent maturity and rate of learning.

Children with handicaps. There are many elements in Piaget's theory and method that suggest its usefulness in appraising the progress of the child who is slow or retarded in his learning, regardless of whether his deficits are to be attributed to constitutional or environmental factors or some combination of both. The theory also provides clues as to the kinds of experiences that may be compensatory.

Summary

This chapter brings to conclusion several years of study of Piaget's theory and experimentation as it relates to the period of early childhood. Our findings have substantiated certain aspects of Piaget's theory and demonstrated its relevance to the education of the young child. In turn, the theory has stimulated further speculation and raised new questions, both psychological and educational.

As the reader must discern, we have been so captivated by the theory as to tend to view many of the problems of teaching young children and planning their curriculum from a Piagetian stance. But however well the theory may stand the test of further investigation and however much the theory may be modified as research goes on, the method seems to us to promise much for the more effective instruction of the young child.

Piaget's method of experimentation is not an educational panacea. It can be misused. A teacher can run through an experiment, pose a few questions, and continue to teach in a routine and mechanical fashion, untouched by the information he could have gained. But Piaget's materials, unlike many of those currently being prepared for the education of young children, are not intended to circumvent the teacher's attempts to intervene in the child's learning. Rather they should render that intervention more appropriate and more effective.

Appendix

Appendix Table A-1. Intercorrelations for Kindergarten Children

ITEM	N	1	2	M	SD
M. C. School					
Stencil	52	=	.17	3.53	2.42
Vocabulary	52		=	25.05	4.80
L. C. School (Children with adequate language)					
Stencil	32	=	.37	1.22	1.42
Vocabulary	32		=	16.63	4.65

Appendix Table A-2. Intercorrelations for First-Grade Children

ITEM	N	1	2	3	4	M	SD
M. C. School							
Stencil	50	=	.02	.36	.46	3.56	2.02
Vocabulary	50		=	.21	.26	27.84	4.92
Pintner	47			=	.60	118.12	17.65
Reading Readiness	48				=	43.73	6.50
L. C. School (Children with adequate language)							
Stencil	34	=	.05	.62	.60	3.24	2.47
Vocabulary	34		=	.34	.20	20.59	4.36
Pintner	28			=	.61	106.64	20.17
Reading Readiness	30				=	38.08	9.32

Appendix Table A-3. Intercorrelations for Second-Grade Children

ITEM	N	1	2	3	4	5	6	M	SD
M. C. School									
Stencil	50	=	.31	.25	−.04	.04	.10	5.92	2.84
Vocabulary	50		=	.41	.44	.41	.35	29.72	5.92
Pintner	46			=	.50	.22	.34	113.65	15.17
Reading Growth	44				=	.26	.56	3.47	.88
Math Concepts (Premeasurement)	48					=	.33	35.63	2.43
Math Concepts (Numerical)	48						=	31.05	4.30
L. C. School (Children with adequate language)									
Stencil	31	=	.03	−.17	−.16	.22	.16	4.29	3.46
Vocabulary	31		=	.26	.48	−.15	−.15	23.71	6.96
Pintner	29			=	.64	.20	.47	106.76	18.72
Reading Growth	29				=	.07	.30	2.87	1.03
Math Concepts (Premeasurement)	30					=	.21	32.32	4.89
Math Concepts (Numerical)	30						=	27.27	5.73

Appendix Table A-4. Raw Scores for Conservation in Longitudinal Study
(Score of 0 or 1 on each of three tasks): M. C. School

| SUBJECT | TESTING DATE | | | | | M | SD |
	Fall 1961	Spring 1962	Fall 1962	Spring 1963	Fall 1963		
108	3	3	3	3	3	3.0	0.0
109	3	3	3	3	3	3.0	0.0
139	3	3	3	3	3	3.0	0.0
120	2	3	3	3	3	2.8	0.4
130	2	3	3	3	3	2.8	0.4
101	3	2	2	3	3	2.6	0.5
104	2	2	3	3	3	2.6	0.5
141	2	2	3	3	3	2.6	0.5
143	2	2	3	3	3	2.6	0.5
145	1	3	3	3	3	2.6	0.8
149	2	2	3	3	3	2.6	0.5
116	2	3	3	2	2	2.4	0.5
112	1	2	2	3	3	2.2	0.7
119	1	1	3	3	3	2.2	1.0
128	0	2	3	3	3	2.2	1.2
134	2	2	2	2	3	2.2	0.4
106	1	1	2	3	3	2.0	0.8
118	2	2	2	1	3	2.0	0.6
121	2	2	2	1	3	2.0	0.6
135	1	2	2	2	3	2.0	0.6
146	1	2	3	1	3	2.0	0.8
137	1	2	2	2	2	1.8	0.4
124	0	2	1	3	3	1.8	1.2
132	0	3	1	2	3	1.8	1.2
102	1	0	3	2	2	1.6	1.0
105	1	2	2	1	2	1.6	0.5
144	2	2	1	2	1	1.6	0.5
100	1	0	2	2	2	1.4	0.8
115	0	1	1	2	3	1.4	1.0
131	1	0	1	2	3	1.4	1.0
147	1	2	1	1	2	1.4	0.5
136	1	1	2	0	3	1.4	1.0
113	0	0	1	2	3	1.2	1.2
117	2	2	1	1	0	1.2	0.7
129	1	0	1	2	2	1.2	0.7
110	0	0	2	1	2	1.0	0.8
138	1	1	1	0	2	1.0	0.6
142	0	0	1	1	3	1.0	1.0
111	0	0	0	0	3	0.6	1.2
123	0	1	0	1	1	0.6	0.5
125	0	0	1	1	1	0.6	0.5
Group M	1.2	1.6	2.0	2.0	2.6	1.8	
SD	1.0	1.0	0.9	1.0	0.7		2.0

Appendix Table A-5. Raw Scores for Conservation in Longitudinal Study
(Score of 0 or 1 on each of three tasks): L. C. School

| SUBJECT | TESTING DATE | | | | | | |
	Fall 1961	Spring 1962	Fall 1962	Spring 1963	Fall 1963	M	SD
452	2	3	3	2	3	2.6	0.5
442	1	2	2	3	3	2.2	0.7
476	1	2	2	2	3	2.0	0.6
404	1	1	1	3	3	1.8	1.0
410	1	1	1	2	2	1.4	0.5
412	1	2	1	1	2	1.4	0.5
447	0	1	1	2	3	1.4	1.0
456	1	1	0	3	2	1.4	1.0
408	0	0	1	2	3	1.2	1.2
429	1	1	2	1	1	1.2	0.4
401	0	1	2	1	1	1.0	0.6
443	0	0	2	2	1	1.0	0.8
417	2	0	1	1	1	1.0	0.6
403	1	0	0	1	2	0.8	0.7
413	1	0	0	2	1	0.8	0.7
421	0	0	2	1	1	0.8	0.7
448	0	1	1	1	1	0.8	0.4
471	1	1	1	0	1	0.8	0.4
432	0	0	1	2	1	0.8	0.7
434	0	0	1	1	1	0.6	0.5
444	1	0	1	0	1	0.6	0.5
449	0	1	0	2	0	0.6	0.8
415	0	0	0	1	1	0.4	0.5
436	1	0	0	0	1	0.4	0.5
Group M	0.6	0.8	1.0	1.5	1.6	1.1	
SD	0.6	0.8	0.8	0.8	0.9		1.3

Table A-6. Standard Scores[a] for Conservation in Longitudinal Study
(Score of 0 or 1 on each of three tasks): M. C. School

| | TESTING DATE | | | | | SUM OF STANDARD SCORES |
SUBJECT	Fall 1961	Spring 1962	Fall 1962	Spring 1963	Fall 1963	
108	6.87	6.36	6.08	6.04	5.54	30.89
109	6.87	6.36	6.08	6.04	5.54	30.89
139	6.87	6.36	6.08	6.04	5.54	30.89
120	5.82	6.36	6.08	6.04	5.54	29.84
130	5.82	6.36	6.08	6.04	5.54	29.84
104	5.82	5.38	6.08	6.04	5.54	28.86
141	5.82	5.38	6.08	6.04	5.54	28.86
143	5.82	5.38	6.08	6.04	5.54	28.86
149	5.82	5.38	6.08	6.04	5.54	28.86
101	6.87	5.38	5.00	6.04	5.54	28.83
145	4.77	6.36	6.08	6.04	5.54	28.79
116	5.82	6.36	6.08	5.00	4.18	27.44
119	4.77	4.42	6.08	6.04	5.54	26.85
128	3.72	5.38	6.08	6.04	5.54	26.76
134	5.82	5.38	5.00	5.00	5.54	26.74
112	4.77	5.38	5.00	6.04	5.54	26.73
106	4.77	4.42	5.00	6.04	5.54	25.77
146	4.77	5.38	6.08	3.96	5.54	25.73
118	5.82	5.38	5.00	3.96	5.54	25.70
121	5.82	5.38	5.00	3.96	5.54	25.70
135	4.77	5.38	5.00	5.00	5.54	25.69
124	3.72	5.38	3.92	6.04	5.54	24.60
132	3.72	6.36	3.92	5.00	5.54	24.54
137	4.77	5.38	5.00	5.00	4.18	24.33
102	4.77	3.45	6.08	5.00	4.18	23.48
105	4.77	5.38	5.00	3.96	4.18	23.29
144	5.82	5.38	3.92	5.00	2.81	22.93
131	4.77	3.45	3.92	5.00	5.54	22.68
136	4.77	4.42	5.00	2.92	5.54	22.65
115	3.72	4.42	3.92	5.00	5.54	22.60
100	4.77	3.45	5.00	5.00	4.18	22.40
147	4.77	5.38	3.92	3.96	4.18	22.21
113	3.72	3.45	3.92	5.00	5.54	21.63
129	4.77	3.45	3.92	5.00	4.18	21.32
142	3.72	3.45	3.92	3.96	5.54	20.59
117	5.82	5.38	3.92	3.96	1.44	20.52
110	3.72	3.45	5.00	3.96	4.18	20.31
138	4.77	4.42	3.92	2.92	4.18	20.21
111	3.72	3.45	2.83	2.92	5.54	18.46
125	3.72	3.45	3.92	3.96	2.81	17.86
123	3.72	4.42	2.83	3.96	2.81	17.74

[a] Distribution has a mean of 5.00 and a standard deviation of 1.00.

Table A-7. Standard Scores[a] for Conservation in Longitudinal Study
(Score of 0 or 1 on each of three tasks): L. C. School

| | TESTING DATE | | | | | SUM OF STANDARD SCORES |
SUBJECT	Fall 1961	Spring 1962	Fall 1962	Spring 1963	Fall 1963	
452	7.46	7.68	7.46	5.58	6.56	34.74
442	5.68	6.46	6.23	6.74	6.56	31.67
476	5.68	6.46	6.23	5.58	6.56	30.51
404	5.68	5.24	5.00	6.74	6.56	29.22
412	5.68	6.46	5.00	4.42	5.44	27.00
410	5.68	5.24	5.00	5.58	5.44	26.94
456	5.68	5.24	3.77	6.74	5.44	26.87
447	3.90	5.24	5.00	5.58	6.56	26.28
429	5.68	5.24	6.23	4.42	4.34	25.91
417	7.46	4.02	5.00	4.42	4.34	25.24
408	3.90	4.02	5.00	5.58	6.56	25.06
401	3.90	5.24	6.23	4.42	4.34	24.13
443	3.90	4.02	6.23	5.58	4.34	24.07
471	5.68	5.24	5.00	3.26	4.34	23.52
413	5.68	4.02	3.77	5.58	4.34	23.39
403	5.68	4.02	3.77	4.42	5.44	23.33
421	3.90	4.02	6.23	4.42	4.34	22.91
448	3.90	5.24	5.00	4.42	4.34	22.90
432	3.90	4.02	5.00	5.58	4.34	22.84
444	5.68	4.02	5.00	3.26	4.34	22.30
449	3.90	5.24	3.77	5.58	3.22	21.71
434	3.90	4.02	5.00	4.42	4.34	21.68
436	5.68	4.02	3.77	3.26	4.34	21.07
415	3.90	4.02	3.77	4.42	4.34	20.45

[a] Distribution has a mean of 5.00 and a standard deviation of 1.00.

Bibliography

Arthur, Grace. A non-verbal test of logical thinking. *J. consult. Psychol.*, 1944, 8, 33–34.

Balinsky, B. In O. K. Buros (Ed.), *The fourth mental measurements yearbook*. Vol. 4. Highland Park, New Jersey: Gryphon Press, 1953, 359.

Barker, R. G., & Wright, H. F. *One boy's day*. New York: Harper, 1951.

Barker, R. G., & Wright, H. F. *Midwest and its children*. New York: Row, Peterson, 1955.

Beard, R. M. The nature and development of concepts. *Educ. Rev.* (Birmingham), 1960, 13, 12–26.

Beilin, H. Perceptual-cognitive conflict in the development of an invariant area concept. *J. exp. child Psychol.*, 1964, 1, 208–226.

Beilin, H., & Franklin, Irene C. Logical operations in length and area measurement: age and training effects. *Child Develpm.*, 1962, 33, 607–618.

Braine, M. S. Piaget on reasoning: a methodological critique and alternative proposals. In W. Kessen & Clementina Kuhlman (Eds.), Thought in the young child. *Monogr. Soc. Res. child Develpm.*, 1962, 27, No. 2 (Whole No. 83). Pp. 41–64.

Brison, D. W. Acquisition of conservation of substance in a group situation. Unpublished doctoral dissertation, Univer. of Illinois, 1964.

Bruner, J. S. *The process of education*. Cambridge: Harvard Univer. Press, 1960.

Bruner, J. S. The course of cognitive growth. *Amer. Psychologist*, 1964, 19 (1), 1–15.

Cheng Tsu-hsin, & Lee Mei-ke. An investigation into the scope of the conception of numbers among 6–7 year old children. *Acta psychol.* (Sinica), 1960 (1), 28–35. (*Psychol. Abstr.*, 35: 4710)

Chittenden, E. A. The development of certain logical abilities and the child's concepts of substance and weight: an examination of Piaget's theory. Unpublished doctoral dissertation, Teachers Coll., Columbia Univer., 1964.

Churchill, Eileen M. The number concepts of the young child: part 1. *Researches and Studies*. (Leeds Univer.) 1958. (a)

Churchill, Eileen M. The number concepts of the young child: part 2. *Researches and Studies*. (Leeds Univer.) 1958. (b)

Churchill, Eileen M. *Counting and Measuring*. Toronto: Univer. of Toronto Press, 1961.

Dodwell, P. C. Children's understanding of number and related concepts. *Canad. J. Psychol.*, 1960, 14, 191–205.

Dodwell, P. C. Children's understanding of number concepts: characteristics of an individual and of a group test. *Canad. J. Psychol.*, 1961, 15, 29–36.

Dodwell, P. C. Relations between the understanding of the logic of classes and of cardinal number in children. *Canad. J. Psychol.*, 1962, 16, 152–160.

Elkind, D. Children's discovery of the conservation of mass, weight and volume: Piaget replication study II. *J. genet. Psychol.*, 1961, 98, 219–227. (a)

Elkind, D. The development of quantitative thinking. *J. genet. Psychol.*, 1961, 98, 36–46. (b)

Estes, Betsy. Some mathematical and logical concepts in children. *J. genet. Psychol.*, 1956, 88, 219–222.

Flavell, J. H. Historical and bibliographic note. In W. Kessen & Clementina Kuhlman (Eds.), Thought in the young child. *Monogr. Soc. Res. child Develpm.*, 1962, 27, No. 2 (Whole No. 83). Pp. 5–18.

Flavell, J. H. *The developmental psychology of Jean Piaget*. Princeton: D. Van Nostrand, 1963.

Fujinaga, T., Saiga, H., & Hosoya, J. The developmental study of the children's number concept by the method of experimental education. *Jap. J. educ. Psychol.*, 1963, 11, 18–26. (*Child Develpm. Abstr.*, 38, 95)

Hagen, Elizabeth P. A factor analysis of the Wechsler Intelligence Scale for Children. Unpublished doctoral dissertation, Columbia Univer., 1952.

Harker, Wilda H. Children's number concepts: ordination and cardination. Unpublished M. A. thesis, Queens Univer., Kingston, Ontario, 1960.

Hill, Shirley A. A study of logical abilities of children. *Dissert. Abstr.*, 1960–61, 214, 3359.

Hood, Blair H. An experimental study of Piaget's theory of the development of number in children. *Brit. J. Psychol.*, 1962, 53, 273–286.

Hunt, J. McV. *Intelligence and experience*. New York: Ronald Press, 1961.

Inhelder, Bärbel. Some aspects of Piaget's genetic approach to cognition. In W. Kessen & Clementina Kuhlman (Eds.), Thought in the young child. *Monogr. Soc. Res. child Develpm.*, 1962, 27, No. 2 (Whole No. 83). Pp. 19–40.

Inhelder, Bärbel. *Le diagnostic du raisonnement chez les débiles mentaux.* (2e éd. augmentée) Neuchâtel: Delachaux et Niestlé, 1963.

Inhelder, Bärbel, & Piaget, J. *The growth of logical thinking from childhood to adolescence.* New York: Basic Books, 1958.

Inhelder, Bärbel, & Piaget, J. *The early growth of logic in the child.* New York: Harper & Row, 1964.

Isaacs, Susan. *Intellectual growth in young children*. London: Routledge & Kegan Paul, 1930.

Kagan, J., Moss, H. A., & Sigel, I. E. Psychological significance of styles of conceptualization. In J. C. Wright & J. Kagan (Eds.), Basic cognitive processes in children. *Monogr. Soc. Res. child Develpm.*, 1963, **28**, No. 2 (Whole No. 86).

Kessen, W. "Stage" and "structure" in the study of children. In W. Kessen & Clementina Kuhlman (Eds.), Thought in the young child. *Monogr. Soc. Res. child Develpm.*, 1962, **27**, No. 2 (Whole No. 83). Pp. 65–86.

Lovell, K. *The growth of basic mathematical and scientific concepts in children*. London: Univer. of London Press, 1961.

Lovell, K., & Ogilvie, E. A study of the conservation of substance in the junior school child. *Brit. J. educ. Psychol.*, 1960, **30**, 109–118.

Lovell, K., & Ogilvie, E. A study of the conservation of weight in the junior school child. *Brit. J. educ. Psychol.*, 1961, **31**, 138–144.

Lunzer, E. A. Some points of Piagetian theory in the light of experimental criticism. *J. child Psychol. Psychiat.*, 1960, **1**, 91–202.

Mannix, J. B. The number concepts of a group of E.S.N. children. *Brit. J. educ. Psychol.*, 1960, **30**, 180–181.

Navarra, J. G. *The development of scientific concepts in a young child: a case study*. New York: Bureau of Publications, Teachers Coll., Columbia Univer., 1955.

Noro, S. Development of the child's conception of number. *Jap. J. educ. Psychol.*, 1961, **9**, 230–239. (*Child Develpm. Abstr.*, **38**, 115)

Oakes, M. E. *Children's explanations of natural phenomena*. New York: Bureau of Publications, Teachers Coll., Columbia Univer., 1947.

Piaget, J. *The child's conception of physical causality*. New York: Humanities Press, 1951. (a)

Piaget, J. *The child's conception of the world*. London: Kegan Paul, 1951. (b)

Piaget, J. *The child's conception of number*. London: Routledge & Kegan Paul, 1952. (a)

Piaget, J. *The origins of intelligence in children*. New York: International Univer. Press, 1952. (b)

Piaget, J. *The construction of reality in the child*. New York: Basic Books, 1954.

Piaget, J. *Play, dreams and imitation in childhood*. New York: W. W. Norton, 1962.

Piaget, J. Cognitive development in children: the Piaget papers. In R. E. Ripple & V. N. Rockcastle (Eds.), *Piaget rediscovered: a report of the conference on cognitive studies and curriculum development*. Ithaca: School of Educ., Cornell Univer., March, 1964. Pp. 6–48.

Piaget, J., & Inhelder, Bärbel. *Le développement des quantités chez l'enfant*. Neuchâtel: Delachaux et Niestlé, 1941.

Price-Williams, D.R.A. A study concerning concepts of conservation of quantities among primitive children. *Acta Psychol.*, 1961 (18), 297–305.

Smedslund, J. The acquisition of conservation of substance and weight in children. I. Introduction. *Scand. J. Psychol.*, 1961, 2, 11–19. (a)

Smedslund, J. The acquisition of conservation of substance and weight in children. II. External reinforcement of conservation of weight and of the operations of addition and subtraction. *Scand. J. Psychol.*, 1961, 2, 71–84. (b)

Smedslund, J. The acquisition of conservation of substance and weight in children. III. Extinction of conservation of weight acquired "normally" and by means of empirical controls on a balance scale. *Scand. J. Psychol.*, 1961, 2, 85–87. (c)

Smedslund, J. The acquisition of conservation of substance and weight in children. IV. An attempt at extinction of the visual components of the weight concept. *Scand. J. Psychol.*, 1961, 2, 153–155. (d)

Smedslund, J. The acquisition of conservation of substance and weight in children. V. Practice in conflict situations without external reinforcement. *Scand. J. Psychol.*, 1961, 2, 156–160. (e)

Smedslund, J. The acquisition of conservation of substance and weight in children. VI. Practice on continuous versus discontinuous material in conflict-situations without external reinforcement. *Scand. J. Psychol.*, 1961, 2, 203–210. (f)

Suppes, P. *Sets and numbers.* Stanford: Stanford Univer., 1961.

Tanner, J. M., & Inhelder, Bärbel. (Eds.) *Discussions on child development.* The proceedings of the first meeting of the World Health Organization study group on the psychological development of the child. Geneva, 1953. Vol. 1. New York: International Univer. Press, 1953.

Thompson, Helen. Adaptive behavior. In A. Gesell *et al., The first five years of life: a guide to the study of the preschool child.* New York: Harper & Bros., 1940.

Vinacke, W. E. *The psychology of thinking.* New York: McGraw-Hill, 1952.

Wallach, Lise, & Sprott, R. L. Inducing number conservation in children. *Child Develpm.*, 1964, 35, 1057–1072.

Wechsler, David. *Wechsler Intelligence Scale for Children.* New York: Psychological Corp., 1949.

Wheeler, Dorothy. Studies in the development of reasoning in school children: I. General methods and results. *Brit. J. statist. Psychol.*, 1958, 11, 137–159.

Whiteman, M. Intelligence and learning. *Merrill-Palmer Quart. Behav.*, 1964, 10, 297–308.

Wohlwill, J. F. A study of the development of the number concept by scalogram analysis. *J. genet. Psychol.*, 1960, 97, 345–377.

Wohlwill, J. F. Development and measurement. In R. E. Ripple, & V. N. Rockcastle (Eds.), *Piaget rediscovered: a report of the conference on cognitive studies and curriculum development.* Ithaca: School of Educ., Cornell Univer., March, 1964. Pp. 95–100.

Wohlwill, J. F., & Lowe, R. C. Experimental analysis of the conservation of number. *Child Develpm.*, 1962, 33, 153–169.

Woodward, Mary. Concepts of number of the mentally subnormal studied by Piaget's method. *J. child Psychol. Psychiat.*, 1961, 2, 249–259.

Worcester, D. A. In O. K. Buros (Ed.), *The third mental measurements yearbook.* Vol. 3. New Brunswick, New Jersey: Rutgers Univer. Press, 1949, 255.

Zimles, H. A note on Piaget's concept of conservation. *Child Develpm.*, 1963, 34, 691–695.